PHILADELPHIA
City of Music

OTHER BOOKS BY JAMES ROSIN

PHILLY HOOPS
The SPHAS and the Warriors

ROCK, RHYTHM & BLUES
A Look at the National Recording Artists
from the City of Brotherly Love

PHILADELPHIA *City of Music*

JAMES ROSIN

Camino Books, Inc.
Philadelphia

Printed in Canada.

1 2 3 4 5 09 08 07 06

Library of Congress Cataloging-in-Publication Data

Rosin, James.
  Philadelphia : city of music / James Rosin.
    p. cm.
  Includes bibliographical references (p.   ) and discography (p.   ).
  ISBN-13: 978-1-933822-00-6 (alk. paper)
  ISBN-10: 1-933822-00-7 (alk. paper)
  1. Philadelphia soul (Music)—Pennsylvania—Philadelphia—History and criticism.
2. Rock music—Pennsylvania—Philadelphia—1961-1970—History and criticism. 3.
Rock music—Pennsylvania—Philadelphia—1971-1980—History and criticism. 4. Rhythm
and blues music—Pennsylvania—Philadelphia—1961-1970—History and criticism. 5.
Rhythm and blues music—Pennsylvania—Philadelphia—1971-1980—History and criticism. 6. Musicians—Pennsylvania—Philadelphia. I. Title.

  ML3477.8.P45R67 2006
  781.6409748'11—dc22   2006004131

ISBN-13: 978-1-933822-00-6
ISBN-10: 1-933822-00-7

Cover and interior design: Jan Greenberg
Cover photographs:
Center, *top*, Billy Paul. Courtesy Blanche Williams
Left to right, Dee Dee Sharp, the Orlons, the Dovells. Courtesy ABKCO / www.abkco.com

This book is available at a special discount on bulk purchases for promotional, business, and educational use.

Publisher
Camino Books, Inc.
P.O. Box 59026
Philadelphia, PA 19102

www.caminobooks.com

Eddie Holman, William Hart, and

Russell Thompkins Jr.

Their inspired vocals have withstood the test of time

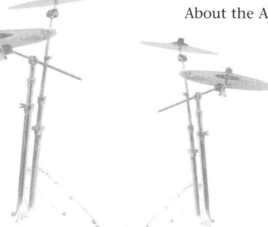

When it comes to the sound of Philadelphia, the beat of the Jersey Shore, and the music that has touched the hearts of millions of people, there are few better writers than James Rosin.

The book you're holding in your hand right now is one you won't want to put down. I thought that Jim's first book (*Rock, Rhythm & Blues*) was a very entertaining and enjoyable journey back to the musical scene of the '50s and early '60s in the City of Brotherly Love. Now I have another book to help me with facts and stories, and make my life as host of a nationally syndicated radio show a lot easier. Filled with information and pictures of the recording artists we grew up with, James Rosin's gift to us is the result of his interviews with these performers. They yield insightful anecdotes and points of view from the pop, rock, and R&B era of the '60s and '70s.

Are you ready to take the "Expressway to [the] Heart" of Philly? "Betcha by Golly [you'll say] Wow," because "The Love [you've] Lost" has been found in this book. Now even "Mrs. Jones" has no need to be a "Lonely Girl." She can take this book on the "Love Train" or to the disco, "Where Happy People Go." From "Cowboys to Girls," the question will be asked: "Could It Be I'm Fallin' in Love" all over again with *Philadelphia: City of Music*?

JIMMY JAY

Host, *The Rewind Show*
Quincy, Massachusetts
www.rewindshow.com

I want to thank all of the people who took the time to share their insights with me: Lee Andrews, Thom Bell, James Darren, Russell Thompkins Jr., William Hart, Billy Paul, Bunny Sigler, Charlie Ingui, Richie Ingui, Ken Jeremiah, Jimmy Ellis, Lawrence Brown, Steven Epstein, Weldon McDougal III, Joe Tarsia, Lloyd Parks, Jerry Blavat, Lou Costello, Bob Bosco, Harold Watkins, Ed Cermanski, Ali Hackett, Stephen Caldwell, Al "Caesar" Berry, Jonathan P. Casey, and David J. Steinberg.

Thanks, too, to Michael G. Silver of Steinberg Business and Music Advisory Services Ltd.; Jody Klein, Teri Landi, Janessa Gursky, and ABKCO Music and Records; Temple University's Urban Archives; Oscar Arslanian; Sal Angelo; and Val Shively and Chuck Dabagian at R&B Records.

For certain biographical entries and information in this book, I would like to acknowledge the following primary sources: All Music Guide, All Media Guide, and their writers, Jason Ankeny (for Linda Creed, Kenny Gamble, the Volcanos, Clara Ward), John Bush (for the Roots), Eugene Chadbourne (for George Ballard), Bruce Eder (for Richard Barrett, Danny Cedrone, Diane Renay), Stephen Thomas Erlewine (for Joan Jett, the Spinners), Andrew Hamilton (for the Epsilons, the Exceptions, the Futures), Ed Hogan (for First Choice, Evelyn "Champagne" King, Bunny Sigler, Three Degrees), Steve Huey (for Boyz II Men, Garnet Mimms, the O'Jays), Chris Kelsey (for Charles Ventura), Steve Leggett (for the Ethics), William Ruhlman (for John Coltrane, Blue Magic, Vivian Green, Jill Scott), Richie Unterberger (for the Ambassadors, Honey and the Bees, Kit Kats), Ron Wynn (for Brenda and the Tabulations, McFadden and Whitehead, the Trammps), Scott Yanow (for Stan Getz, Grover Washington Jr.); History of Rock (www.historyofrock.com/rhythm_and_blues.htm); R&B Music Primer (www.rhythmandtheblues.org.uk); and Wikipedia, the free encyclopedia (www.en.wikipedia.org).

I also wish to express my appreciation to my publisher, Edward Jutkowitz of Camino Books, and my editor, Barbara Gibbons.

Finally, thanks to the friendly folks in Wildwood, New Jersey, who have embraced the past and supported my writing: first and foremost, Lori and Paul Russo of Cool Scoops Ice Cream Parlor (in North Wildwood), where you can step back in time with wonderful '50s and '60s music, antiques, and memorabilia, while enjoying tasty sundaes in a '57 Chevy, '57 Ford, or '59 Cadillac car booth; the Greater Wildwood Chamber of Commerce; the Wildwood Historical Society; Mayor Ernie Triano, a man with a vision; newspaper columnist Jim Vanore; and La Piazza, a warm and friendly restaurant, where South Philadelphia's Joey M sings the sounds of Sinatra.

AUTHOR'S NOTE

I have made a responsible effort to make sure that information such as names, dates, titles, statistics, discographies, and other facts are correct. Where discrepancies exist, I have, whenever possible, gone to original sources—record labels, the artists themselves, and those closely associated with the music industry during the period covered in the text—to resolve them.

The glue that brought us together
and keeps us together
is our love of music.
So respect each other,
because respect creates
power, honesty, and strength.
Don't abuse the music.
Give it the respect
it needs to grow.

— Kenny Gamble

Philadelphia during the '60s and '70s was a power-house center for pop music. Whether it applies to an individual, or an entire city, it's not how heavy you are, but how long you're heavy!

— Kal Rudman

CITY OF MUSIC

CHAPTER ONE
Rhythm and Blues
The Early Years

Rhythm and blues first took root in the Deep South, at the turn of the century, coming to us in a musical form called the blues. Expressing the feelings and emotions of black musicians in rural areas of Mississippi and Alabama, this music was conveyed through song, sometimes accompanied by resonating guitar strings and harmonicas. In many ways, the blues echoed the hardships of the migrant working-class people.

Artists such as Ma Rainey, Ida Cox, and Bessie Smith made the first blues recordings in the 1920s. In the 1930s, as millions of black southern workers migrated to the North in search of a better tomorrow, blues music became more urbanized and sophisticated.

A lively and entertaining saxophonist who played a major role in the urbanization of the blues was Louis Jordan. Coming to Philadelphia in the 1930s from Arkansas, he worked with local bands and began a solo career in 1938. It was Jordan, along with musicians like Count Basie and Lionel Hampton, who bridged the gap between the big band and R&B eras of the 1940s. He became a prime architect for what became known as the jump blues, played by smaller versions of the swing band. These combos consisted of six to eight musicians who played piano, bass, electric guitar, drums, and both alto and tenor sax. The music was up-tempo, spirited, cheerful, and rambunctious, with a boogie-woogie backbeat. The featured soloists were usually the two wailing sax players, who matched the energy of the music and took the spotlight.

As the larger swing bands began to wane, jump blues bands began to flourish. From 1942 through 1951, Louis Jordan had 57 hits on Decca Records alongside pop singer luminaries Bing Crosby, Frank Sinatra, and Ella Fitzgerald.

♩ **Lou Costello (WVLT FM 92.1: Cruisin' with the Oldies):** When you heard the captivating beat and alluring sound of artists like Louis Jordan and Wynonie Harris, it drew you from your seat to your feet. Even when I play their music today on my Wednesday night show *(The Doo-Wop Diner)*, I can't help but clap my hands and stamp my feet right there in the D.J. booth. Much of this music is timeless. Good is good, regardless of what the calendar says.[1]

Leon Mitchell (music director, Philadelphia Legends of Jazz Orchestra): In the mid-'50s when I arrived at a professional stage as an arranger, my cousin, Hammond organist Harry "Doc" Bagby, referred Louis Jordan to me, to do some arrangements. My first paid assignment was "Saturday Night Fish Fry." I was curious to know if there was such a thing. Louis assured me there was and invited me to one in the 4400 block of Sansom Street in Philadelphia. While there, Louis convinced me to try some chitlins. Everyone raved about them. I did and thought they tasted really great. Later that night, someone told me that chitlins are hog bowels, and I never ate them again to this day. At later fish fries, I stuck to the fish or chicken and, boy, were they some great parties![2]

In the postwar era, other prominent R&B artists who achieved great success as a result of Louis Jordan were Big Joe Turner, Wynonie Harris (mentioned opposite), and Roy Brown. Turner was a large, loud, and colorful performer whose career spanned forty years. Some of his greatest hits were "Flip Flop and Fly," "Corina, Corina," and "Midnight Special."

Harris was a handsome, brash, and highly intelligent entertainer, who knew how to manipulate his audience. His first solo hit was the 1947 "Playful Baby," followed by hits like "Bloodshot Eye" and "Oh Babe" (written by Louis Prima).

Roy Brown was a teenage crooner in the Bing Crosby mold, who became successful in the late 1940s with hits like "Good Rockin' Tonight."

The infectious rhythm and emotional intensity of this music could not be denied. In 1947, Jerry Wexler at *Billboard* magazine created a new category to coexist with pop music, called "rhythm and blues." The early center of recorded rhythm and blues was in Los Angeles and later spread to Chicago, St. Louis, Detroit, and Memphis.

By the early to mid-'50s came such artists as Ruth Brown, Laverne Baker, Ray Charles, Clyde McPhatter, and Chuck Willis—all showcased in the R&B roster that Atlantic Records developed—whose work, in turn, inspired 1960s and '70s classic soul.

CHAPTER TWO

Rock 'n' Roll

A New Variation

In the late 1940s and early 1950s, many teenagers sought their own musical identities. Not content to listen to the pop singers their parents fancied—Bing Crosby, Perry Como, Frank Sinatra, Rosemary Clooney, Frankie Laine, and Patti Paige—they began listening to the R&B stations. This alarmed many white middle-class Americans, who felt the lyrics of R&B (called race music) were sexual, or suggestive, and might corrupt the morals of their sons and daughters.

Weldon Arthur McDougal III (songwriter, producer, public relations representative): I would say some of the lyrics in early R&B music were a play on sex. A lot of the time the lyrics would shift gears and you'd find out the vocalist was making references to something that had nothing to do with sex. For example, a lyric like "baby, let me bang your box" may sound suggestive, but then a few bars later, you find out the box is a guitar or piano.[1]

Lee Andrews (recording artist): The idea that the R&B music of that time, in itself, was sexual and suggestive in nature was a misconception. Much of the music was really a free expression of rhythm and emotion; something we all have inside us that's not particular to any race or color. It's a basic part of humanity. Instead of embracing that, the white middle class was fearful and shied away from it. At the same time, the youth desired to hear more of it, and understand what it was. But because they were not allowed to accept it, they began to create variations in their mind—a likeness of what they thought they were hearing. This variation is what came to be known as "rock 'n' roll." The term had been coined in the R&B era, perhaps even earlier, but popularized in the late 1950s by D.J.s like Alan Freed. Rock and roll was an assimilation of the R&B music heard in the black culture. It became an interpretation of such that was deemed acceptable to the white culture.[2]

McDougal III: What's ironic is that R&B music wasn't written for or intended for the black audience. It was wonderful music with rhythm, written for people to enjoy. But in reality, the only people who you could sell it to were blacks, given the nature of the times. You couldn't go to white middle-class America and say, "What do you think of this?" But if people around you were satisfied with your product, you knew what you were able to do with it.

In the early rock and roll years, the music establishment would smooth out parts of the sound and lyrics of R&B, to make them more familiar and acceptable to middle-class America. Themes like family values, teen love, and car obsessions, expressed through innocuous lyrics, were the norm.

Bill Haley and His Comets (the first white rock 'n' roll band to tap into the musical mainstream) recorded their first million-seller in 1954: "Shake, Rattle and Roll," a covered version of the R&B hit by Big Joe Turner.

Lou Costello: Some of the covered versions by white artists were recorded line by line with much the same arrangement. When they did that, it opened the doors for kids like me to discover the R&B vocalists and gravitate toward their music. The covered versions simply didn't have the feel that the originals had.[3]

Bob Bosco (writer, *Echoes of the Past*): It was also not unusual for record companies to produce an album with all black artists, but have a cover with white kids dancing to their music at a hop, or listening to it at a pajama party.[4]

Andrews: What brought about the more contemporary rhythm and blues era were black youths such as myself who clung to groups like the Ink Spots and the Mills Brothers. Ironically, they sang more in the pop music vein and cut back on their rhythm. From those two groups came the Orioles, Ravens, Five Keys, Bill Ward and the Dominos, and the 5 Royales in the early '50s. They, in turn, begat groups like the Drifters, Platters, Flamingos, Coasters, and Lee Andrews and the Hearts. On the other side, you had the birth of Elvis Presley, Everly Brothers, Jerry Lee Lewis, and Buddy Holly, who emulated us. As you look back at music history, that situation always existed. The answer to Fats Waller, Louis Armstrong, and Dixieland was Jimmy Dorsey, Glen Miller, and Bob Eberle. There was always a counter move in the white music culture to the blues, spirituals, and R&B in the black community. Then in the late 1950s, an interesting thing happened. Black artists like Chuck Berry, Jackie Wilson, and Sam Cooke began to cross over into the pop area, and vice versa. So if you look back at the whole picture, the two sides that had been created for the wrong reasons created a wide umbrella of music that the public gathered behind. Maybe that was God's way of putting forth a variety for us to love, enjoy, and call America's music!

Philadelphia became the City of Music in the 1950s. Music historians marvel at the enormous talent pool that emerged from the City of Brotherly Love and the Greater Philadelphia Area, giving rise to pop, rock, and R&B artists, from various musical backgrounds, who achieved national prominence. Bill Haley and His Comets, from nearby Chester, Norristown, and Upper Darby, opened the musical doors for many other performers. South Philadelphia fostered prerock pop artists such as Al Martino, Eddie Fisher, Gloria Mann, Sunny Gale, Georgie Shaw, and Joe Valino. (Mario Lanza went to Hollywood and became a star at MGM.) With the advent of rock 'n' roll came Charlie Gracie, Frankie Avalon, Fabian, Bobby Rydell, Chubby Checker, and James Darren. Out of Southwest Philly, West Philly, and

Overbrook Park came Lee Andrews and the Hearts, Danny and the Juniors, the Orlons, the Dovells, Dee Dee Sharp, the Tymes, Solomon Burke, and Patti LaBelle. Beloved local groups, such as Anthony and the Sophomores, the 4 J's, and Billy and the Essentials, also thrived.

James Darren (recording artist, actor, director): People ask me what was it about South Philadelphia that gave rise to so many performers and entertainers. I can't say exactly. I would say South Philadelphia was unique in the sense that everyone not only knew each other, but looked out for and helped each other. It was an extremely tight-knit community with roots from Market Street to League Island Park, and from 25th Street to Front Street. You always got strong support from your friends and people in the neighborhood. And when someone became successful, it gave all of us inspiration.[5]

Record labels, like Swan, Jamie-Guyden, and Chancellor, flourished in Philadelphia. Cameo-Parkway became the most productive and influential independent record company in town, producing over 130 Top-100 hits between 1957 and 1967. *American Bandstand* with Dick Clark, originating from WFIL Studio at 46th and

Market (in West Philadelphia), played a huge part in allowing teens all over the country to listen to the same music at the same time.

The music industry had to listen, too. All of a sudden there were 13 million teenagers with voices of their own that legitimized the emergence of rock 'n' roll. The excitement and abandon of the music encouraged teens to step outside the constraints of the '50s. The transistor radio, portable record player, and 45 rpm facilitated this growing freedom.

Charlie Gracie (recording artist): The early rock 'n' roll music was all about the backbeat and melody. The lyrics were almost incidental in my opinion. The only true lyricist at that time was Chuck Berry. To me he was the great poet of rock 'n' roll because his lyrics told a story.

In the early days, rock 'n' roll was great dance music with a fresh sound. That's because we recorded it live, unlike today, and we'd do take after take until we got it right. We had no one to emulate. We started it all. Our music was the bottom of the pyramid of everything that was to follow. We set the trend of what was to come and last to this day.[6]

Darren: What's interesting is that early rock 'n' roll and R&B music from the '50s and early '60s is still going strong. You have music with simple lyrics, basic chords, and harmony that's lasted for 50 years. It's still played all over the country, not just by people who discovered it, but by today's young people as well.

Rhythm and blues, the blueprint and cornerstone of rock 'n' roll began to broaden its horizons as well. A number of Philadelphia R&B recording artists, including Lee Andrews and the Hearts, the Sensations, Turbans, Silhouettes, Dreamlovers, and Solomon Burke, gained national acclaim on the pop charts.

Al "Caesar" Berry (The Tymes): In the early 1960s, Philadelphia reigned supreme. Cameo-Parkway was like Motown. We had in-house artists that would back up other artists, such as Bobby Rydell, Chubby Checker, and Dee Dee Sharp. It was a big happy family and everyone did what was expected of them. We went from singing on the street corner to the big time. So it didn't matter where we fit in. Just being a part of the musical process was a true sense of joy to all of us.[7]

CHAPTER THREE

Philly in the British and Motown Years

In 1964, the music industry began to change rapidly, and Philadelphia would feel the effects. British rock groups began to take over. With their records climbing the charts, they dominated the airwaves.

♪ **Joe Tarsia (chief engineer, Cameo-Parkway):** Sweeping social change took place in the mid-'60s. One day, guys came to work in shirts and ties, and the next in sandals, shorts, and long hair. Journeymen musicians were replaced by self-contained groups that mimicked the British Invasion. Pop music as we knew it literally collapsed. The Beatles did that. Who wanted to buy music written by adults for teens when they could listen to and buy music written by their peers? It didn't touch the same kind of nerve.[1]

♪ **Bunny Sigler (recording artist, songwriter, producer):** I remember Bernie Lowe [owner of Cameo-

Parkway] saying [the Beatles will] be gone in a couple of months. No one thought they'd achieve the success that they did. But the Beatles weren't just artists that someone wrote songs for. They were extremely talented and creative musicians that wrote great music. I had never heard some of the sounds that went into their tracks. Listen to "Sgt. Pepper's Lonely Hearts Club Band," and you realize what a phenomenon they were. I can remember them singing "Yesterday" on the Ed Sullivan Show. A week later it had sold a million copies.[2]

♪ **David J. Steinberg (Steinberg Business and Music Advisory Services):** When I was a young attorney, Cameo-Parkway was one of our clients. The distributor for Cameo-Parkway in England was EMI. EMI had released Beatles records in the U.S. on MGM, VJ, and Swan, all of which were unsuccessful. Then EMI offered some new Beatles releases to Bernie Lowe and I advised him to take them. These Beatles records were beginning to chart in the U.K. But the business advisors at Cameo-Parkway urged Bernie to decline the offer. Shortly after, EMI gave those releases to Capitol Records [in the U.S.] and within a few months the Beatles became a worldwide success. The older Beatles records on MGM, Swan, and VJ were re-released and became big hits in the U.S. as well. I believe that if Cameo-Parkway had become involved with the English sound, which swept the country, they could have become one of the most powerful record companies in the U.S., if not the world. Instead, it signaled their downfall.[3]

♪ **Jonathan P. Casey (WSNJ AM):** Around early 1964, the demand for Beatles music was so strong that any record label that had ever recorded a song by the Beatles immediately released it. That same year, the Beatles had five hits on five different labels. Swan Records, a Philadelphia label, had the rights to "She Loves You (Yeh, Yeh, Yeh)" and immediately suspended pressing material of any other artist in development in favor of the Beatles. Multiply that scenario and you see how devastating it was to the American artist. Bobby Rydell, one of Cameo-Parkway's most successful recording stars, had recorded "World Without Love" (written by Paul McCartney). Expectations were high when it hit the charts, but the song was covered by England's Peter and Gordon (which rose to Number 1) and Bobby's version was overshadowed by the mania for British recording artists.[4]

♪ **Stephen Caldwell (The Orlons):** In 1964, we had three charted songs: "Shimmy, Shimmy," "Rules of Love," and "Knock Knock." When it looked like they might take off, the British invaded our musical shores and the page of *Billboard's* American artists went blank. One week we were on the charts and the next we were gone.[5]

♪ **Jerry Blavat (Geator Gold Radio Network):** It became increasingly difficult for established recording artists in this country to get airtime. By the mid-'60s, 60 percent of the average playlist on radio were groups like the Beatles, Rolling Stones, Dave Clark Five, Jerry and the Pacemakers, Herman's Hermits, Peter and Gordon, Chad and Jeremy, and Freddy and the Dreamers.[6]

The British Invasion and departure of *American Bandstand* signaled the end of Cameo-Parkway Records. In 1964, Chubby Checker was the only artist to have a Top-40 charted hit. The company lost heavily, and, in 1965, Bernie Lowe sold his controlling interest to a group of investors. In 1967, the company was sold again to Allen Klein, who closed its doors. One of the last artists to have a hit on Cameo-Parkway was Bunny Sigler.

♪ **Sigler:** When "Let the Good Times Roll" came out, I was out in California. In those days, the impact of a hit record on the East Coast wouldn't reach the West Coast until a month later. I was on the beach in Malibu and heard the song on the radio. I remember jumping up and running around telling everyone to turn up their radios: "That's My Song." I came back to Philly and felt like I was on top of the world. I had a hit record and I started working everywhere. With my name, everyone thought I was Jewish. But when I got there, they thought I was the bodyguard and wanted to know where Bunny was. I didn't disappoint them. I had something for everyone. I sang "Hava Nagila" in Hebrew, arias in Italian, and love ballads in French, in addition to pop and soul. I had a great time on stage and so did my audience. Then one day I got a call, and the royal carpet was pulled out from beneath my hit song. Cameo-Parkway had closed up. All the promotion men (both national and local) that had worked on the record were taken off it. "Let the Good Times Roll" had reached Number 12 on the pop charts and had a shot at going to the top. Now stations began to stop playing it. Not only the pop stations, but the R&B ones as well. What a turn of events. But the song never died and I still work on it. As late as last year I was in England, and I sang "Let the Good Times Roll" and five other songs from the album. When I did them, those people were in heaven, just hearing them. They knew every word of each song and even the "ooh's" and "ahh's" in between.

Apart from the obvious British successes, a standout organization in the music world was Motown Records. Founder Berry Gordy Jr., with a highly creative and talented staff of songwriters, arrangers, producers, and musicians, built one of the most impressive rosters of recording artists in pop music history. The cast included Mary Wells, the Marvelettes, Martha Reeves and the Vandellas, Smokey Robinson and the Miracles, the Four Tops, the Temptations, the Supremes, Stevie Wonder, Marvin Gaye, and Tammi Terrell.

With songs written by Holland, Dozier, Holland and Smokey Robinson, these artists were backed by a group of studio musicians known as the Funk Brothers, who shaped the Motown sound. They included Joe Hunter, Earl Van Dyke, and Johnny Griffith (piano); Robert White, Joe Messina, and Eddie Willis (guitar); James Jamerson and Bob Babbitt (bass); Benny Benjamin, Richard "Pistol" Allen, and Uriel Jones (drums); Jack Ashford (percussion and vibes); Herbie Williams (trumpet); Hank Crosby (sax); and Paul Riser (trombone).

Motown music of the mid-'60s was a more refined take on what kids were looking for. More elaborate and polished, the sound attracted an older audience as well, whereas mostly teenagers were drawn to doo-wop and earlier forms of rock 'n' roll.

♪ **Lee Andrews:** The country was ready for a change, and Motown was the conductor waving the baton in another direction. I'm still amazed at its birth and development. America loved and embraced their music, and it spread across the world. It truly touched your very soul.[7]

♪ **Joe Terry (Danny and the Juniors):** Motown had a great formula. They could take a commonplace, everyday expression like "Sugar Pie Honey Bunch" (Four Tops) or something metaphorical like "Tracks of My Tears" (Smokey Robinson and the Miracles) and create a wonderful song with magical rhythm that influenced all of us.[8]

♪ **Weldon Arthur McDougal III:** Motown brought us a brand-new beat with universal appeal. It touched everyone with a unique rhythm. You could hear it in the instrumental and vocal elements of each song. Most important, it was bona fide dance music.[9]

Bubbling under Motown and the British Invasion was the R&B community in Philadelphia. Weldon Arthur McDougal III (who created the Larks), Johnny Stiles, and Luther Randolph formed a production company (Dynodynamics) and their own record label (Harthon Records). They were recording hits at Frank Virtue's studio, above a furniture store on North Broad Street near Columbia Avenue. (D.J. Jimmy Bishop of WDAS was also involved and recorded some of their songs on his Arctic label.)

It was here that a teenage songstress named Barbara Mason wrote and recorded a song called "Yes, I'm Ready." Some feel her sultry and soulful voice embodied the style of what would become the "Sound of Philadelphia."

♪ **Ali Hackett ("King of the Oldies"):** The message in Barbara's music was simply stated with pure feeling. Her love ballads were a true relief amidst the civil unrest, Vietnam War, and drug culture of the time. Her music spirited us into young adulthood and made us all think about responsibility.[10]

♪ **McDougal III:** After we did the track and Barbara did the vocals for "Yes, I'm Ready," arranger Russ Faith heard the results and offered to do the arrangement for free. Then I recruited Don Renaldo, who brought in the string section from the Philadelphia Orchestra to "sweeten the sound." When it was done, I played the record back and wasn't sure what we had. It sounded so different. Around the corner from Harthon Records was a record shop at 60th and Market. So I took the record over there for the owner to play. The next day he wanted to buy a whole box because people liked it. At that point, we were off and runnin'.

McDougal, Stiles, and Randolph also produced a group called the Volcanos and a young falsetto out of Overbrook High School named Eddie Holman.

♪ **McDougal III:** Eddie Holman was originally a songwriter for Harthon Records. When he demonstrated his work, his voice caught our attention and we suggested he record.

Out of these recording sessions came "Storm Warning" (Volcanos) and "This Can't Be True Girl" (Holman). The rhythm section for Dynodynamics con-sisted of the talented and reliable Norman Harris (guitar), Ronnie Baker (bass), Earl Young (drums), and Luther Randolph (keyboard). Harris, Baker, and Young later became the core of MFSB, the house band at Philadelphia International Records.

Much of R&B, as it evolved from the 1950s on into the '60s and early '70s, became known as soul music. Many of the soul artists found broader appeal with the white audience, unlike the R&B pioneers of earlier days. Whereas some saw rock 'n' roll as a white interpretation of rhythm and blues, soul music, in its fusion of blues, R&B, and gospel, was driven by raw vocal power fueled by frank emotion. In the 1950s, Garnett Mimms, Ray Charles, and James Brown (the Godfather of Soul) were early examples of soul artistry, followed by Solomon Burke in the early '60s.

There were variations and different approaches to soul music. Motown was considered lighter, rhythmic, and more pop-oriented, with broad appeal. Southern soul in places like Memphis (Stax Records) and Muscle Shoals, Alabama, had a different character. The South attracted an array of artists, such as Otis Redding, Wilson Pickett, Percy Sledge, and Aretha Franklin (the Queen of Soul).

Sigler: Southern soul had a more driving, straight-ahead style, with more of a hard rhythm. Sometimes their rhythmic sounds resembled a herd of elephants. Another element was their horn players didn't necessarily read music and played in unison notes. With Philly soul, our musicians read the arrangements, played the horn lines, the harmony lines, and gave it a different sound.

McDougal III: Soul music is basically music that you feel. If you walked into a crowded black bar and sat there, you'd observe some people come in off the street, hear the music being played, and groove to it. They automatically start walkin' that beat. Something in the music touches their soul and they respond to it, like something was burnin' their feet. That's what sets it apart from other forms of music. And it's not exclusive to the black community. Listen to the Righteous Brothers' version of "You Lost That Lovin' Feeling." Fabulous. They hit the right groove with the right words. You could feel it. It puts the chills through you. That's soul music!

In the mid- to late '60s, Kenny Gamble and Leon Huff joined forces and became a prolific and successful songwriter–producer team in Philadelphia. Huff, from Camden, was a gifted piano player and songwriter, who had worked on a number of recording sessions in Philadelphia and New York. Gamble, who grew up in West Philadelphia, was a baritone with music in his soul. Early on, he worked as a session singer, who sang background vocals for artists such as Barbara Mason.

The pair first worked together in the early '60s as members of the Romeos, a group that Gamble and Thom Bell had created. (When Bell left, Huff replaced him). In 1964, they collaborated on "The 81," a single by Candy and the Kisses.

Tarsia: Kenny was driven by music. It pulled him in like a magnet. Wherever it was he was. There's an old story that when Kenny was in his teens, he was walking down the street and heard a song he really liked coming from someone's house. So he went up to the house, rang the doorbell, and asked the people what the song was.

Sigler: Kenny's music came from the heart. He could sing you the melodies, you'd hear the chords, add more chords, and it all came together. Kenny and Leon could sometimes write 10 songs in a day.

♫ **Charlie and Richie Ingui (Soul Survivors):** Kenny and Leon were definitely men with a vision. They really believed the world should be like the lyrics in their music. Something that transcended black and white. The beauty of their music is that it had universal appeal.[11]

In the mid-'60s, Gamble and Huff created their own label, Gamble Records, and teamed up with a group called the Intruders. Sam "Little Sonny" Brown, Eugene "Bird" Daughtry, and Robert "Big Sonny" Edwards sang together on street corners and were also part of a gospel group in the late '50s. However, the teenage trio were not exactly choirboys and earned their professional name from crashing parties in the neighborhood. A fourth member, Phil Terry, joined the group, and they began recording in the early '60s. Most of their songs went unheralded until 1965, when they recorded "Gonna Be Strong" for Gamble and Huff. Jimmy Bishop gave "Gonna Be Strong" good airplay, and the record began to sell locally. Their next effort, "(We'll Be) United," hit the pop charts, and their third recording, "Together," rose to Number 48. Several more charted songs followed through 1967; then the group enjoyed their greatest suc-cess with "Cowboys to Girls" (a Number-1 R&B hit, Number 6 on the pop charts).

♫ **Tarsia:** "Cowboys to Girls" was a song with broad appeal. It dealt with growing up, going from childhood games to young adulthood, and reflecting on the difference. I can hear Little Sonny's voice right now. It was very unique. He was a perfect example of someone with a very interesting and entertaining sound that wasn't always on pitch and skirted the notes a bit. But Kenny once said to me, "There are a lot of great singers, but I look for voices with character." That's the essence of people like Eddie Lavert (of the O'Jays) and Teddy Pendergrass. You could pick those voices out of a thousand singers because they were very distinctive. Little Sonny was probably the best example of that because his voice was a tenor with a little bit of gravel in it. That gave it texture.

The group would record another nine charted songs through 1974, mostly all written and produced by Gamble and Huff (on Gamble Records). Their most notable successes were "(Love It like a) Baseball Game" (1968), and "I'll always Love My Mama (Part 1)" (1973).

The Intruders became one of the first R&B groups that gave rise to Philly soul.

In 1967, Crimson Records, a local company owned by Jerry Greene, Jared Weinstein, Jerry Blavat, and Nat Siegel, hired Gamble and Huff as independent producers, because of their regional success with the Intruders.

Crimson had signed a New York group called the Soul Survivors. The group created quite a stir in Philadelphia with their appearances at the Living Room (a club at 13th and Locust). The group consisted of vocals, Charlie and Richie Ingui and Kenny Jeremiah, and two musicians, Joseph Furgione and Paul Venturini.

Charlie Ingui: We were fresh and different. The songs we did were very danceable, and our visual appearance had as much to do with our appeal as our music did. Being from New York, we would shop for our clothes in Greenwich Village. They were very hip for the time and a style people in Philadelphia were not accustomed to.

Ken Jeremiah (Soul Survivors, 1966–1969): By the time we opened at the Living Room in Philly, we'd created this big buzz. Within a short period of time, there were lines around the block and every night we sold out. They were charging seven bucks to get in, which was unheard of at that time. Not only were they getting in, but we were drawing people from all over the Delaware Valley. This led to a guest spot on the *Jerry Blavat Show*, where we went on and played live.[12]

Blavat: I liked their sound and when I heard something that appealed to me, I would go with my heart and not the research charts. I also had a policy on the show where no one would lip-sync. When Lloyd Price, Fats Domino, and Little Richard were guests, they brought in their musicians. James Brown had a whole busload. It didn't matter. So the Soul Survivors fit right in. They came on, brought their band, and sang live. In fact, the reaction was so good, I had them on every week.

Blavat recommended the group to Gamble and Huff, who went to see them perform. After that, they set up a meeting.

Charlie Ingui: Kenny and Leon played a song for us they were working on called "Expressway to Your Heart." They wanted to see if we were the right group. So we sang it with two leads, Richie and I, which Kenny loved—something he would later do with the O'Jays. I really believe that's the way he envisioned the song. The second time we met, the song was done, and we went into the old Cameo-Parkway studio to record it. Joe Tarsia was the engineer; Kenny and Leon produced. In addition to our band—Paul, Joe, and Chuck Trois—Leon played piano, and Winnie Wilford, from Kenny's former group the Romeos, played bass.

Jerry Greene (Crimson and Lost Nite Records): The production cost for Expressway was $309.00. The original version was four minutes long, which was an unacceptable length on AM stations in 1967. Fortunately, Kenny and Leon were creative and flexible. They were able to reduce the length to 2:21. Maybe one day we'll release the original version.

Some of the best-remembered characteristics of the recording were the honking horns and traffic noise.

Tarsia: At Cameo, when we took a group like the Orlons and did their greatest hits, or hits of their peers on an album, there would always be some little shtick with sounds. So I keyed on having the producers give the record some kind of identity that set it apart from the rest. While we were doing "Expressway," it seemed natural to have those sounds in it. So I went to the music store and bought a sound-effects record with horn sounds.

Charlie Ingui: I believe the first time "Expressway to Your Heart" got airplay was June of '67. But it wasn't until October that it peaked. It got to Number 4 on the pop charts and Number 3 on R&B. But the song reached Number 1 in every market it played. In those days, you didn't have the instant distribution and promotion you have now. The record was built from city to city by promo reps on the street.

Jeremiah: Initially, most of the stations that played us were R&B stations. In Philadelphia, WDAS and WHAT were the first radio stations to play it, and both Georgie Woods and [Joe] "Butterball" [Tamburro] really pushed it. After it got noticed, WIBG and WFIL joined in.

Richie Ingui: Most people didn't know we were a white group. You didn't have the recognition factor of MTV back in the late '60s. We toured for years and people never knew.

♪ **Charlie Ingui:** On occasion, a promoter would try to get out of his contract with us; sometimes even cancel our engagement. They were unsure what the reaction would be from the black audience. For example, we were set to perform at Newark's Paramount Theatre in the middle of the 1967 riots. It was an all-black show with Jackie Wilson as the headliner.

♪ **Richie Ingui:** That week, "Expressway" was Number 1 on WWRL, which was "the R&B station" in New York. By the evening show, they were rioting in the streets, and the National Guard was mobilized. So Jackie Wilson decided to go on first and get out of there. Usually when the headliner finishes, people start leaving, and there's no telling how these people would react. When Jackie finished, people were out of their seats. But we were waiting around all day and determined to go on. Our guitar player was new and shakin' like a leaf. His amp was way on the other side of the stage. So I told him, "As soon as you get to that amp, plug in and start 'Expressway.' Don't wait for anyone else to kick in." Usually we would end up with that song. That night we began with it. Well, we began playing and they loved us. They were dancin' in the aisles.

♪ **Charlie Ingui:** As I look back at "Expressway," it really was a good record and well put together. That pounding baseline was catching, and the horns and piano in the intro were so identifiable.

♪ **Richie Ingui:** I think anybody that ever lived near traffic in an urban area could relate to it.

The Soul Survivors' next song, "Explosion in My Soul," was also a hit and charted at Number 30.

♪ **Charlie Ingui:** The custom then was to capitalize on your previous hit. We were on a ride, and our thought was to keep going. But in reality, "Explosion" sounded too similar to "Expressway" and never achieved the same success.

Ironically, some music critics felt the group's third recording, "Mission Impossible" (later released as "Impossible Mission"), was their best effort, and termed "a perfect balance of psychedelic and soul."

♪ **Richie Ingui:** Unfortunately, we were told there was a conflict of interest with the television series, *Mission Impossible*, and that either the studio or the network threatened legal action. That signaled the end of what might have been a great record.

In 1969, the Soul Survivors moved to ATCO Records and reconnected with New York. Musicians Furgione and Venturini left the group. Later that year, Ken Jeremiah left and formed a group called Roman Candle.

In 1974, the Inguis were contacted by Gamble and Huff. They were asked to record a song that Gamble and Huff had written called "Soul to Soul." The result led to a new album called *The Soul Survivors*, released on TSOP (a subsidiary label of Philadelphia International). Using their newly formed rhythm section, the group wrote most of their songs, which blended pop with R&B and included the popular cut, "City of Brotherly Love." This was the Soul Survivors' final collaboration with Gamble and Huff.

CHAPTER FOUR

The Maestro and the Lyricist

Along with Kenny Gamble and Leon Huff, Thom Bell would become known for creating the Sound of Philadelphia.

Bell was born in Philadelphia on January 27, 1943, and grew up in a musical household. His mother played piano and organ; his father, accordion and pedal–steel guitar; and his four brothers, tenor sax, baritone sax, guitar, and keyboard. His sister played piano and danced ballet. By the time Bell was four, he played drums, and, from age six on, learned piano.

♪ **Thom Bell:** I was in the second grade in Miss Mosley's class, and even then music was always on my mind. One day I was looking out the window and engrossed in music. Miss Mosley noticed I wasn't paying attention to her teachings and wanted to know what I was paying attention to. I told her I was listening to music. She suggested I stand up and share it with the class. So I did. I gave them the violins here, the drums there, and before I knew it, I was in the school nurse's office giving her the same recital. When I finished, she dispatched me to the principal. He wanted to know if I had problems at home, wouldn't take my word for it, and summoned my mother. That was his misfortune. After he got done telling her what he thought was wrong with me, he awakened the Jamaican wrath within her soul and she laid him out right there on the spot. Then she made him deliver a written apology for calling her son crazy for hearing what was a regular event in her family's household, and pulled me out of that school. But I learned my lesson. From then on, I kept all the music inside my head and never let anyone in on it until the time was right. To this day![1]

While in high school, Bell played at his sister's dance recitals and other social events to earn money. By the time he was 17, Bell played seven different musical instruments, but still favored piano and drums.

♪ **Bell:** Any really good musician can play piano because if you play trumpet, sax, trombone, flute, or oboe, you can play one note at a time. With piano you can play 10 notes at a time, because you have 10 fingers. So when you play chords, you can hear the contrasting harmonic notes at the exact same time as the note you play with your instrument. It's then that you hear the beauty of those notes and your note fit together. What I've learned in composing melodies is when a sound intrigues you, it feels pleasant, like sitting on a cushion. If it's good, it caresses your ear, goes inside, and stays there. It becomes part of your memory. For most people, a good sound will stay with you all the time. Most people prefer to stay in that plane of thinking. If it's not good or it's unpleasurable, you leave it behind so you don't step on it. Hence the old saying, "Your behind follows your mind."

Bell began playing piano in New York, Philadelphia, and Baltimore theaters behind Jerry Butler and the Impressions, the Dells, and other prominent artists on what was called the "Chitlin Circuit."

Finding that he disliked duplicating other people's music, Bell began writing songs with Kenny Gamble, whom he met and befriended through his sister. In 1958, Gamble and Bell formed a singing group called Kenny and Thommy, which recorded a song called "Someday." Several years later, they created a rhythm section called the Romeos, including Roland Chambers (guitar), Karl Chambers (drums), Winnie Wilford (bass), Bell (piano), and Gamble (lead vocal).

In 1962, Bell became musical director for Chubby Checker. Cameo-Parkway, in 1964, decided to create an in-house black rhythm section to compete with Motown, so Bell was placed in charge and became the arranger and conductor. The band included Roland Chambers (guitar), Winnie Wilford (bass), Cliff "Chester Slim" Jackson (drums), and Bell (keyboards). When Cameo-Parkway was sold in 1965, Bell became an in-house producer with the new regime.

In 1966, a group called the Delfonics was brought to Bell's attention by their manager, Stan Watson, who owned a record store and tow truck business in West Philadelphia. The group consisted of two singers and three musicians. Bell didn't care much for the two vocalists, but was impressed by the high tenor voice of guitarist William Hart, who also wrote songs for the group. When two members quit, William, his brother Wilbur, and their friend Randy Cain became the Delfonics. Their first recording was "He Don't Really Love You" (written by William Hart).

♪ **William "Poogie" Hart (lead singer and songwriter):** I was very concerned about the songs I wrote. I wanted to write what I felt were beautiful love songs, that would cross over and draw the attention of the pop market as well. I didn't want them to sound black or white. I wanted them to be songs for everyone, as Barry Manilow would say, "for the whole world to sing." That became my concept of songwriting and the way I write to this day.[2]

"He Don't Really Love You" was released on Moon Shot, a small affiliated label. The record did well locally, but the company made no special effort to promote it. However, based on the local reaction, Cameo-Parkway asked Bell and Hart to produce another Hart song, entitled "You've Been Untrue," and released it on their label. The song received good airplay from D.J.s Jimmy Bishop, Joe "Butterball" Tamburro, and Georgie Woods, but, again, the record was not promoted well. (Less than two years later, Cameo-Parkway was sold again and closed operations.) "Poogie" Hart and Thom Bell remained undaunted, and, in 1967, Hart wrote a love ballad called "La La Means I Love You." Bell did a great arrangement of Hart's melody with rhythm and strings. Stan Watson was

so impressed with the result that he formed a record label called Philly Groove to release it. "La La Means I Love You" was a huge R&B hit, rose to Number 4 on the pop charts, and put the Delfonics on the map.

♪ **Hart:** "La La Means I Love You" was a very personal song to me. When my first son was born he would say, "La la la la." I thought baby language was very sincere, and I assumed he was telling me that he loved me. Then it hit me, "La La Means I Love You." I also felt it would grab people's attention. "La La" is the root order of all songs. When someone isn't sure of a lyric they sing "La la la la." The word just flows with music and has a lot of power to it.

Through 1968 and 1969, the Delfonics had six more charted songs, including the re-release of "He Don't Really Love You." Then, in early 1970, came one of their most memorable tunes: "Didn't I (Blow Your Mind This Time)," penned by "Poogie" Hart. The song was a Top-10 hit, sold a million copies, and won the group a Grammy for Best R&B Vocal Performance. (The song was later re-recorded by New Kids on the Block in the late '80s and won Song of the Year.)

♪ **Hart:** "Didn't I (Blow Your Mind This Time)" was based on my relationship with a girlfriend who continually did me wrong and thought she had me in place. But one day I had enough of it, and said something she never expected to hear. Hence the lyrics:

> *Ten times or more*
> *Yes, I walked out the door.*
> *Get this thing through your head,*
> *There'll be no more.*[3]

I blew her mind that time!

Later that year, Bell parted ways with Stan Watson and the Delfonics. He went back to doing arrangements for Gamble and Huff.

♪ **Hart:** Thom was a great musician, producer, and arranger. He was easy to work with and we had a great chemistry. He was classically trained and went by the book. I did not. But he was music-savvy enough to sense my songs and chord changes worked. Even if I didn't understand the mechanics the way he did, he respected my lyrics and melodies and never stepped on them. Instead, he took what I offered and built on it. Thom Bell played a very important part in creating our classic sound.

The Delfonics would go on to record charted pop songs on Philly Groove such as "Trying to Make a Fool Out of Me," "When You Get Right Down to It," "Somebody Loves You," and "Ready or Not, Here I Come." (Major Harris replaced Randy Cain in 1971.)

The Delfonics, with William Hart's high tenor signature paved the way for many other artists. Today they are seen as one of the more imitated vocal groups in the music industry.

Linda Creed, lyricist extraordinaire, grew up as an R&B child of the '60s in the Mt. Airy section of Philadelphia. Her kinship with music led to an early singing career locally. With Frankie Beverly and the Butlers as her backup band, she sang at places like the Convention Center and the Arena.

During a respite from performing, Creed moved to New York and worked for a music publisher. It was there she became friends with funk singer Sly (of Sly and the Family Stone), who recognized her talent and creativity. Sly encouraged Creed to sing and write songs.

♪ **Steven Epstein (former vice president of promotions for United Artists; former head of East Coast promotions and special promotions and** development for Atlantic Records): Linda didn't like the fast-paced lifestyle of New York and chose to move back to Philadelphia. So she called her father and said, "Tell someone to meet me. I'm comin' home." (That became the basis for the hit song "I'm Comin' Home," about her life in New York, later recorded by Johnny Mathis and covered by the Spinners.)[4]

Back in Philadelphia, Creed became friends with Randy Cain, who was working with Thom Bell, and Cain introduced the pair.

Bell asked Creed if she could write songs. Unsure but interested, Creed came to Bell's office the next day and was given a melody. She took it home and wrote the lyrics to a song that became "Free Girl," later recorded by Dusty Springfield. Bell and Creed developed an instant rapport and began to work together.

♪ **Epstein:** Thom was a musical genius. He would hum a melody to Linda, and in his mind he heard the end result. He knew the entire orchestration: strings, horns, everything. Linda would take it home, write the lyrics to his syncopation, and bring it back to him.

About a year after Bell parted company with the Delfonics, he was introduced to a group called the Stylistics.

♪ **Epstein:** The Stylistics had recorded a song called "You're a Big Girl Now" in 1971. That became a "mid-charter." So the group was picked up by Avco Records. The original producers [of "You're a Big Girl Now"] were somewhat inexperienced, so the executives at Avco contacted Thommy and asked him to listen to the group.

Bell was very impressed with the group's lead singer, a personable young man named Russell Thompkins Jr., and agreed to work with them. Thompkins, with a pure and sweet falsetto, became the driving force of the Stylistics, and Bell built the music around him. One of the first things that Thompkins began to do after working with Bell was to lower his register.

♪ **Russell Thompkins Jr. (lead singer, the Stylistics, 1971–2000; lead singer, Russell Thompkins and the New Stylistics, 2003–):** I'm very happy that Thommy brought my key down. As I grew older, I was still able to sing those songs in the same key because I didn't sing at my maximum vocal range in the earlier years. One of the reasons he did that was when he and Linda wrote the songs, they did it in the key he sang at. So when he showed me the songs, they were in his vocal range, which brought my voice down to the same range as his. That worked well. It was still a comfortable area for me, and where he wanted me in his composition.[5]

Bell and Creed's first effort for the Stylistics was "Stop, Look, Listen (to Your Heart)" released in June of 1971. It sold 900,000 copies and climbed to Number 3 on the R&B charts. This was followed by a succession of eleven charted hits, including five gold releases: "You Are Everything" (1971), "Betcha by Golly Wow" (1972), "I'm Stone in Love with You" (1972), "Break Up to Make Up" (1973), and "You Make Me Feel Brand New" (1974).

♫ **Thompkins Jr.:** Thom Bell had a wonderful overall sense of what he wanted his music to sound like. There was a real beauty in his orchestrations. If you took the vocals out and simply listened to the musical construction, it was still a treat to hear. He used everything as his instruments to play, not only the rhythm section, strings, and horns, but even the vocals. He knew where he

wanted them to be and how they should sound. At the same time, he gave me artistic leeway to sing the songs the way I wanted as long as I didn't go against key or whatever he had already structured. With Thommy, I was able to develop my own identity in the song. After doing three albums with him, I had a system in place where I could work with any producer on earth. I could sit down with arrangers and piano players, listen to the song one time, and I had it. All I had to do was work out the exact key I'd do it in. I learned all that from Thommy Bell.

That Bell lived and breathed music was not an overstatement.

♫ **Epstein:** Thommy lived at Belmont and Parkside Avenues, and he would walk to work at 309 South Broad Street every day. He did that for about four months. Linda would ask him, "Why are you doing that?" He would say, "There's something in my head and I can't be disturbed or distracted." Then one day I'm driving along, and I see Thommy walking. I honk the horn, he jumps in the car all excited, and hands me a tape to play. It's the melody to "People Make the World Go Round," with him humming. Well, he gives it to

Linda, and she can't get a feel for it. Then, all of a sudden, we're watching Larry Kane on the news, and he says, "The trash men are not going to pick up your trash today. They're on strike." Bang! She's got it.

Trash men didn't get my trash today,
Oh, why? Because they want more pay.[6]

She calls Thommy, sings him the song, and that was it. "People Make the World Go Round" became a Number-1 hit. That was the first time a stand-up R&B group recorded a song that lasted nine minutes. Thommy extended it with instruments doing it with a 4-4 backbeat.

Thompkins Jr.: "People Make the World Go Round" became so popular in the early '70s that radio stations would play the vocal part, then play the music part. In fact, I put a revised version of that song on my new CD, *A Matter of Style*.

In 1972, Bell and Creed would also form a creative and successful union with the Spinners, who became one of the most popular R&B groups of the decade.

Epstein: I was handling East Coast promotions for Atlantic Records and worked closely with the president, Jerry Greenberg, who was a good friend. When he inquired about Thom and Linda's availability, I set up a meeting. Thom was offered the pick of Atlantic's roster, from *A* to *Z*, including some impressive performers like Roberta Flack and Aretha Franklin. But Thommy chose the Spinners.

The Spinners, a Detroit-area group, had their first hit, "That's What Girls Are Made For" (a Top-10 R&B tune in 1961) for Tri-Phi Records, featuring Bobby Smith on vocals. When Motown took over Tri-Phi in the mid-'60s, the Spinners became part of their roster. The group had some R&B hits, including "I'll Always Love You" and "Truly Yours." In 1970, they enjoyed their greatest success with "It's a Shame" (written and produced by Stevie Wonder, featuring lead singer G. C. Cameron).

But Motown never showed a genuine interest in the Spinners and released them in 1971. Shortly after, the group signed with Atlantic Records. Tenor Philippe Wynne replaced G. C. Cameron and the remainder of the group consisted of Bobby Smith (tenor), Billy Henderson (tenor), Henry Fambrough (baritone), and Pervis Jackson (bass).

Bell: Back in the early '60s, when I was a piano player at the Uptown, the Spinners were on the bill and sang an R&B hit they had, called "That's What Girls Are Made For." There was a dissonant chord in that song, a B flat 13 (flat 9), which was hard to play and even harder to sing, and they made it sound effortless. I never forgot that. There I was, years later, going down the list of Atlantic artists I was offered, but none of them jumped out at me. I wanted to work with a group or an artist that I felt really needed me. People like Aretha Franklin and Roberta Flack were doing fantastic. They didn't need me. It was my job to revive the artist and bring them back to where they've been or take them to where I thought they belong. At the very bottom of the list was a crooked word that looked like it said "Spinners." I wondered if that was the group that sang that dissonant chord at the Uptown. Yes, it was; but Atlantic didn't want to give them to me. They were ready to cut them loose. I said, "Give me one shot and if I don't succeed, you can do what you want." They agreed. I went to Detroit to hear the group and told them I'd be back in two weeks with some songs. I returned with three: "How Could I Let You Get Away?" "We Belong Together," and "I'll Be Around" (cowritten with Phil Hurtt). Atlantic put out "How Could I Let

You Get Away" as the *A*-side, and "I'll Be Around" on the *B*-side. I told them they made a mistake and made them a proposition. "You take six weeks on the *A*-side, then give me six weeks on the *B*-side, with my own promotion team, and see what happens." Well, "How Did I Let You Get Away" became a Number-1 R&B hit, but "I'll Be Around" was not only a Number-1 R&B hit, but went to Number 3 on the pop charts.

Epstein: The Spinners gave Thommy a nice option: two bona fide lead singers in Bobby Smith and Philippe Wynne, with great backup. Bobby was a strong tenor who could grab onto a song and make it his own. Philippe was a down-home, soulful motherf—r, and a great ad-libber.

Bell: Bobby had the pop sound and Philippe had the gospel. When I put them together, all the bases were covered. What I didn't know was that Philippe was a singer of that magnitude, which he later showed on songs like "Mighty Love," "Sadie," and "Rubberband Man." I didn't realize how creative he could be. When we recorded "Could It Be I'm Falling in Love," and the song began to have a sameness, I asked Philippe if he could ad-lib toward the end of it. I can still hear his voice: "Okay, Thommy. I'll try." So I told Joe

Tarsia, who was engineering, not to worry about the balance, and put him on a separate track. I knew you'd never get the same thing twice from a gospel-driven singer. Try he did. If we hadn't cut the tape at song's end, he would have kept on going for another half-hour. I never imagined how different Philippe was. Every time we took him into the studio, he revealed something new and gave the Spinners an added dimension. When we did "Then Came You," with Dionne Warwick, Philippe came on late in the song and gave it new life. People in the studio thought we'd started another tune.

♪ **Lee Andrews:** Philippe was a combination of gospel and R&B. His style consisted of melody and syncopated rhythm that gave him a kind of uniqueness in the '70s music market. Everything he sang had his own personal stamp, and it drew people in.[7]

After the huge success of "I'll Be Around" and "Could It Be I'm Falling in Love" in 1972, more gold records followed: "One of a Kind (Love Affair)" (which combined Bobby Smith and Philippe Wynne as alternate leads in 1973), "Then Came You" (with Dionne Warwick in 1974), "They Just Can't Stop It (Games People Play)" (1975), and

"Rubberband Man" (1976), written by Linda Creed, which earned a Grammy award. Other charted Spinners songs penned by Creed include "I'm Coming Home," "Ghetto Child," and "Living a Little, Laughing a Little." However, the principal writers for the group were Joseph B. Jefferson (a versatile vocalist–pianist–drummer), Bruce Hawes (a keyboardist–lyricist–melody writer), and Charles Simmons (lyricist–melody writer). Jefferson wrote "One of a Kind Love Affair" and combined with Hawes and Simmons to produce the hits "Games People Play," "Mighty Love," "Love Don't Love Nobody (Pt. 1)," and "Sadie," featuring Philippe Wynne.

♪ **Bell:** Jefferson, Hawes, and Simmons were a fantastic combination. They were the catalytic agents. They gave me those wonderful songs that spoke to me and told me what to do. It all began when Linda was unable to be there in the beginning with the Spinners and was absent for periods of time. She was getting married and later began raising a family. But her absence led me to Joe, Bruce, and Charles. They became my backbone, support structure, and the main creative energy force.

In addition to the many songs and melodies he wrote, Thom Bell earned a reputation for lush, precise, and detailed arrangements that yielded a beautiful sound.

♪ **Bell:** I wanted to make every note of each melody count. I would strive to make my music not only pleasing to the ear, but exciting from the very start to attract my listeners like a bee to a blossom. If I did my job, then we'd be on the same plane, or the same train, in the same way, on the same day, and arrive together!

Intoxicating introductions, which became a trademark of Bell's work and intrigued his listening audience, distinguished many of his megahit songs that went gold.

♪ **Bell:** In arranging "Didn't I (Blow Your Mind This Time)" I used French horns at the very beginning to signal a call to arms, to grab your attention, as if to say, "Citizens, gather around. We have something to say." The idea came to me from remembering the horns in the film, *The Vikings,* with Kirk Douglas, Tony Curtis, and Janet Leigh. With "Betcha by Golly Wow" [Stylistics], the intro changed keys three times before we came to the verse. I always used the oboe with Russell [Thompkins Jr.] because it enhanced the beauty

in the same octave that he sang. I also used the English horn to augment his vocals, depending on what key he was in. In the intro to "You Make Me Feel Brand New," I used a sitar to emphasize the melody and added brass, strings, and harp to give it a Renaissance feeling.

At the start of "Could It Be I'm Falling in Love," I began with a keyboard and after eight bars brought in full-strength strings and horns. On "One of a Kind (Love Affair)," I used a drum beat to attract both your ear and your body. Nothing fancy, but a beat with a lot of air and breathing room to create a sound that was leading you somewhere; but you'd have to wait to find out. Then came the guitar and you'd wait some more. Then came the orchestra and verse.

During an eight-year period (1968 to 1976), Bell achieved twelve gold records and seven gold albums with the Delfonics, Stylistics, and Spinners. After the release of "Rubberband Man" by the Spinners, Bell had reached the summit (he had likewise reached a peak three years earlier with the Stylistics and, three years previously, with the Delfonics). He then ended his association with the Spinners.

Bell: I could no longer function in the situation I was in. I've always been in this business to make music. I love what I do, but if I can't make a good product, see where my artists are headed, and where they'll be a year from now, it's time to hand the baton to someone else. If you look around at all the music groups, you realize no one person will take them on the entire journey. The time will come when it doesn't feel like it used to, no matter how successful you are. Then you have to be honest with yourself and say, "I've reached that point where I can't go any further in this same direction," and make a change.

That same year Thom Bell and Linda Creed also parted company. In the summer, Bell moved to Washington—where he set up a studio—and would return to Philadelphia on occasion to work with Gamble and Huff, though he remained independent. Throughout the '80s and '90s, he collaborated with artists such as Elton John, Johnny Mathis, Deniece Williams, James Ingram, and Earth, Wind and Fire.

Linda Creed moved to California with her husband, Steven Epstein, who was managing the funk-rock group War. Her independent projects included two albums with Teddy Pendergrass: *Love Language* and *Closer*. From the lat-

ter came "Hold Me in Your Arms," which featured an unknown singer named Whitney Houston. In 1977, Creed teamed with composer Michael Masser to write "The Greatest Love of All" for the Muhammad Ali biopic, *The Greatest*. The song would top the charts for Whitney Houston in 1986. That same year, Creed passed away from breast cancer in her mid-30s.

Epstein: We were unaware of how many people were affected by her talent and artistry. The Eagles credited their sound to Creed and Bell. Isaac Hayes was in awe of Linda. Referring to "People Make the World Go Round," he'd say, "How did that little girl come up with those lyrics to that 4-4 backbeat?" When Paul McCartney met Linda, he said, "In England, you're the Queen." When she met Smokey Robinson, her idol, he was just as impressed as she was.

Bell: If the lyrics were about beauty inside or out, you knew it came from Linda. Every word and syllable meant something to her. We had a great formula. She'd say, "Call me when you're ready, Bell." I still think about her all the time. My parents have a picture of Linda on their wall and say a blessing for her every day. You couldn't help but love her. She was so honest, simple, and real.

Linda Creed is still very much with us through her musical legacy. For many, she truly became "the greatest love of all."

Philippe Wynne left the Spinners in 1977 and was replaced by John Edwards. (Wynne later worked with George Clinton and passed away in 1984.) The Spinners would have two more hits in 1979 and 1980: "Working My Way Back to You Girl/Forgive Me Girl" and "Cupid/I've Loved You for a Long Time." They continued recording through the '80s and eventually entered the oldies circuit.

CHAPTER FIVE
The Sound of Philadelphia

By the late '60s, Kenny Gamble and Leon Huff had made steady progress on the musical horizon. They had produced a total of 10 charted songs for the Intruders (on Gamble Records) and the Soul Survivors (on Crimson), including two megahits: "Expressway to Your Heart" and "Cowboys to Girls." They also produced hits for Jerry Butler ("Only the Strong Survive," "Moody Woman," and "Hey, Western Union Man" on Mercury Records) and for Archie Bell and the Drells ("I Can't Stop Dancing" on Atlantic). In 1969, they created their second record label (Neptune) to release albums and singles through Chess.

Columbia Records took notice of their accomplishments in 1970, offering them the opportunity to create a new affiliated company, and, in early 1971, Philadelphia International Records opened their doors. With Columbia's backing (a $75,000 advance for 15 singles, and LPs budgeted at $25,000 apiece), Gamble and Huff burst onto the national scene with top hits like "Me and Mrs. Jones" by

Billy Paul, "If You Don't Know Me by Now" by Harold Melvin and the Blue Notes (also spelled Bluenotes), and "Backstabbers" and "Love Train" by the O'Jays, selling millions of records. Throughout the 1970s, Philadelphia International continued to score hits with groups like MFSB (Mother Father Sister Brother), the Three Degrees, Lou Rawls, the Jacksons, the Trammps, Teddy Pendergrass, People's Choice, and the Jones Girls (Shirley, Brenda, and Valerie).

Gamble, Huff, and Thom Bell brought a definitive sound, with full, lush orchestration. In their recording sessions, it wasn't unusual to find their ensemble composed of 18 strings, 10 horns, and a rhythm section, with added percussion, which brought the total to 40 to 50 musicians. Their combination of sweeping strings, vibrant horns, and an emphatic rhythm section embodied the Sound of Philadelphia. Their house band, MFSB, consisted of Norman Harris (guitar), Ronnie Baker (bass), Earl Young (drums), Larry Washington (percussion), Zach Zachery (sax), Vince Montana (vibes), Roland Chambers (guitar), Karl Chambers (drums), Bobby Eli (guitar), Richie Rome (piano), Leonard Pakula (keyboard), Don Renaldo (strings and horns), and, later, Ron Kersey (keyboard), T. J. Tindall (guitar), Victor Carstarphen (piano), and Dexter Wansel (keyboard). Many of the arrangements were done by Thom Bell, Bobby Martin, and, later, Jack Faith (a knowledgeable and talented musician–songwriter), who contributed heavily when Thom Bell moved to Washington.

> ♪ **Joe Tarsia:** Out of a mix of people that included Thom, Bobby, Jack Faith, Richie Rome, Roland Chambers, Lenny Pakula, Dexter Wansel, and Victor Carstarphen, Kenny found that various people had different assets. For example, Thom Bell did great strings and Bobby Martin did great horns. So, quite often we'd have two arrangers on a song. Sometimes Kenny did the arrangements. He'd call in an arranger and change things. He'd sit there and hum, and the arranger would feverishly make notes while 10 horn players waited outside. At one point, I set up a blackboard and had it painted with a staff on it. That way, the arrangers could write down the notes, and the musicians could make their changes on their charts.[1]

Philadelphia International had an interesting blend of musical creativity—both schooled musicians and musicians with feel.

> ♪ **Tarsia:** The most important element to Gamble and Huff was the feel and sincerity of the vocals and music. If they got that, and technical perfection was not there, they'd settle for 95 percent. Thom Bell, on the other side, was highly trained and extremely structured. He wrote down every note and nuance and didn't look for spontaneity. He understood every facet of his arrangements. The end result of Thom's work was a well-orchestrated, beautiful sound. Gamble and Huff looked for musicians to interpret. With Norman Harris, Ronnie Baker, and Earl Young, they could well afford that. They were adept at laying down the charts and putting their feel to the music. The riffs and figures Norman and Ronnie played weren't written down. That happened in the studio, and Earl had a relaxation and held a tempo like no drummer I have ever heard. Kenny and Leon would run down the chord chart; these guys would get into the song and feel the music. A lot of what they did was spontaneous. Then they'd take that spontaneity and run it down until they perfected the arrangement.

One of the first blockbuster hits at Philadelphia International was Billy Paul's "Me and Mrs. Jones." Paul was a unique talent, who grew up in Philadelphia and developed a vocal style that incorporated traces of jazz, R&B, and pop. His album, *Feelin' Good at the Cadillac*

Club, attracted Gamble and Huff, who signed Paul to record for Neptune. In 1970, he recorded the album *Ebony Woman*, and, in 1971, his record album *Going East* was released on Philadelphia International.

♫ **Billy Paul:** In 1972, I was cutting the album, *360 Degrees of Billy Paul,* at Philly International. We were about to do the last song when my piano player, Eddie Green, told me that Kenny had a song he wanted me to listen to. It was written by Cary Gilbert, Kenny, and Leon, and called "Me and Mrs. Jones." When I heard it, I liked it but I wasn't sure about it. There were parts that sounded flat to me. So when my wife and I went to St. Thomas for peace and quiet, I took the song with me. I worked on it and added my signature. When we came back, I recorded it and knew we had something special. When I went to Chicago for Jesse Jackson's Operation Breadbasket, I sang the song and got a standing ovation. I never looked at "Me and Mrs. Jones" as a song about adultery. Instead, I romanticized it. I chose to sing about the beauty that two people found in spending time together, in spite of what they were going through.[2]

In the 1970s, at Philadelphia International, Gamble and Huff would enjoy their biggest success with Harold Melvin and the Blue Notes, and the O'Jays. Both groups had common characteristics: they had been around and were not new kids on the block. The Blue Notes began as a group in 1954. Two years later, a 16-year-old named Harold Melvin joined them (replacing one of the members who enlisted). Melvin was a second tenor, who also wrote songs and did choreography. The Blue Notes' first recording, "If You Love Me," was a regional hit, and, in the late '50s, they recorded "My Hero" (from Broadway's *The Chocolate Soldier*), which became a charted hit in 1960. By that time, the group had broken up, and Melvin formed a new Blue Notes, consisting of Melvin, John Atkins (lead vocal), Lawrence Brown, and Bernard Wilson. This group stayed together throughout the '60s, performing in top nightclubs all over the world. In 1965, they had their first R&B charted hit with "Get Out (and Let me Cry)."

♫ **Lawrence Brown (Blue Notes, 1958–1969; Harold Melvin and the Blue Notes, 1971–1975):** Harold had a magnetic personality and a definite way with people. We all worked well together and had a very entertaining act. Our lead singer, John Atkins, was a versatile performer and a great showman. John was heavy-set, but very light on his feet and slid across the stage like a lightweight.[3]

In late 1969, the group broke up. When they got back together in 1971, John Atkins chose not to return, in order to spend more time with his family. Tenor Lloyd Parks joined the group, which was rechristened Harold Melvin and the Blue Notes. When they signed a contract with Philadelphia International, Melvin made a significant move that would ensure the group's success. Teddy Pendergrass, who had been a drummer with the Blue Notes in previous years, was promoted to lead singer.

Brown: Teddy had this very distinctive voice. It was kind of raw, raspy, and soulful, with great range. He could go from a deep baritone to a first tenor. Teddy loved performing and was able to draw from the audience, to make what he did even better.

The group's first success was a mid-chart song, "I Miss You," in the summer of 1972.

Lloyd Parks (Harold Melvin and the Blue Notes, 1971–1974): There was a sadness in "I Miss You," yet it touched base with a lot of people. That had to do with the troubled times of the early '70s, with the war and generation gap in a lot of families. The first part of that song where you hear the high notes was the result of an ad-lib. Phil Terry and I were at the piano, and he suggested I relax and come up with a beginning. Being a high tenor, I hit those high notes; then Teddy came in. It worked well and gave the song a nice touch.[4]

The group next struck gold with "If You Don't Know Me by Now" (written by Gene McFadden and John Whitehead), which became a Number-1 R&B hit and rose to Number 3 on the pop charts.

Brown: "If You Don't Know Me by Now" was a great soulful ballad. Listeners really responded to the parts where you had Teddy pleading over Lloyd's falsetto riffs. That gave the song a humanity that touched a lot of people. I loved the fact that it was done in three-quarter time like a waltz. In fact, after that, I noticed a lot of songs done in three-quarter time would hit the Top 10.

Another huge hit for the group came a year later, in 1973, with "The Love I Lost (Part I)" (also penned by McFadden and Whitehead). This was a significant recording because it helped to usher in the disco age and showed that Harold Melvin and the Blue Notes could achieve success with up-tempo songs.

♫ **Brown:** The interesting thing about "The Love I Lost" was the way it shifted gears. It began with a slight guitar riff, like someone walking down the street without a care in the world. All of a sudden it took off full throttle, with full orchestration, and built from there. When it came to the vocals, Harold, Lloyd, Bernie, and I sang the chorus in unison, in full harmony, and the background became the lead that gave Teddy the freedom to ad-lib and do his thing above and below us.

Both "The Love I Lost" and the equally up-tempo "Bad Luck (Part I)," which broke out in early 1975, solidified the group's place in the world of disco.

♫ **Brown:** As much as I enjoyed "The Love I Lost," my favorite was "Bad Luck (Part I)." To me that song turned the music world around. When you listened to it, it gave you that feeling where you had to move; rock back and forth, and groove with what you heard. The impact of that song was huge. Even comedians like Richard Pryor felt the need to mention it in their comedy albums.

Female vocalist Sharon Paige joined the group in the mid-'70s and helped get them on top of the R&B charts with the duet, "Hope That We Can Be Together Soon." Another huge R&B and pop hit for the group was McFadden and Whitehead's "Wake Up Everybody (Part I)," which peaked at the end of 1975.

♫ **Brown:** "Wake Up Everybody" took an interesting path. At first, it was an unfinished recording. We left it undone and went away on tour for two, three months. The same thing happened with another song of ours, "Satisfaction Guaranteed." But while we were away, we'd work on the song and rehearse it in our dressing room and at the hotel. The longer we lived with it, the more we understood it, and the better things turned out. When we finally recorded it, the end result was our first single to go platinum.

Extended instrumental versions, labeled "Part II," were made for "I Miss You," "The Love I Lost," "Bad Luck," and "Wake Up Everybody."

♫ **Bunny Sigler:** Our album cuts got played on FM stations that weren't governed as much by time as the AM stations were. So we weren't concerned about cutting three-minute songs. We would go in and jam, develop that feel until we got the quality we were looking for. I did a slowed-down version of "Love Train" that was eight minutes long. The D.J.s would call it their "bathroom break" song. Another song, "You Got Your Hooks in Me," ran four minutes. That wouldn't have gotten play on an AM station.[5]

The arranger that was responsible for much of the Blue Notes' work was Bobby Martin.

Brown: Bobby was an awesome arranger and sax player. He could put horn lines together like you wouldn't imagine. He would have almost the entire Philadelphia Orchestra at our sessions. He also had a great facility with people. He could get musicians to do things they didn't think they were capable of doing. He was a jovial guy and a real people person who made everyone laugh. Even in a bad situation.

In late 1975, Pendergrass, Brown, and Wilson left Harold Melvin over financial and creative differences and formed their own Blue Notes group, which featured Pendergrass. (Parks had left earlier.) Sharon Paige remained with Melvin, who replaced the departed

Pendergrass with David Ebo and several others. However, Philadelphia International did not renew Harold Melvin and the Blue Notes' contract.

Recording next for ABC, the group hit the R&B Top 10 in 1977 with the title track of "Reaching for the World." That would prove to be their last commercial success. (Paige and Ebo left the group in 1980.)

The Blue Notes group (composed of Pendergrass, Brown, Parks, and Wilson) remained together for five months. In the spring of 1976, Teddy Pendergrass went solo and became a major recording star for Philadelphia International.

Brown: At the time, our road manager wanted to put Teddy's name out front. He and other people behind the scenes realized what we didn't: that there was a demand for Teddy from his exposure on our albums. But we opted to keep it as a group. Then Teddy left us and, with the same writers, had three hit albums back-to-back. Our decision not to highlight him in the forefront was one we deeply regretted for a long time. As a group, we could always decorate a stage and dazzle an audience with our showmanship, harmony, choreography, and flamboyance. But Teddy added so much to it. Had we all been more business-oriented, and realized the music was the star, it would have turned out differently.

The Blue Notes continued performing together in the '70s and '80s, with John Atkins returning to the group. Today, billed as Harold Melvin's Original Blue Notes, Lawrence Brown and Lloyd Parks are joined by Arthur Aikens, Lenny Edwards, and Salaam Love.

Harold Melvin would reorganize his group and perform throughout the '80s and early '90s. Sadly, in 1996, he suffered a stroke and passed away in 1997 at age 57. But his talent, showmanship, and enterprise are well documented among the R&B community of today. (A new Harold Melvin's Blue Notes group created by Mrs. Harold Melvin was formed in recent years and also appears in concert.)

The O'Jays, like Harold Melvin and the Blue Notes, was a group with a musical track record. Eddie Lavert and Walt Williams were childhood friends in Canton, Ohio. Inspired by Frankie Lyman and the Teenagers, they began singing R&B songs on the radio while attending high school. They recruited classmates William Powell, Bill Isles, and Bobby Massey and, in 1958, formed a group called the Triumphs. (In 1960, they became the Mascots.)

Their initial recording, "Miracles," in 1961, aroused the interest of Eddie O'Jay, an influential Cleveland D.J., who gave them airplay and career guidance. In acknowledgment of his support, the group renamed itself the O'Jays.

In 1963, the O'Jays had their first charted single, "Lonely Drifter," on Imperial Records, followed by "Lipstick Traces (on a Cigarette)" two years later, which rose to Number 48 on the pop charts. Their next two releases charted low, and Bill Isles left the group. The O'Jays switched to Bell Records, in 1967, and recorded "I'll Be Sweeter Tomorrow (Than I Was Today)," which became their first Top-10 R&B hit. But when their next two charted songs were not as successful, the group considered disbanding. The O'Jays then met Gamble and Huff, who had created their new Neptune label. Gamble and Huff liked their sound and believed they were more than a journeyman R&B group.

The O'Jays recorded "One Night Affair," in 1969, their first of three records on Neptune (arranged by Thom Bell and Bobby Martin). The new label was distributed by Chess. Unfortunately, Chess had recently been sold, and the new ownership, GRT (General Recorded Tape), placed little emphasis on smaller record labels. The O'Jays recorded two more charted songs in 1970: "Deeper (In

Love with You)" and "Looky, Looky," but neither received strong promotional effort. Neptune folded that summer, and the O'Jays returned to Ohio. (Bobby Massey left, and the group was then a trio.)

When Philadelphia International opened its doors in 1971, the O'Jays were one of the first groups that Gamble and Huff signed to their label. Their first recording in 1972, "Backstabbers," became a Number-1 R&B hit, received a Grammy nomination, and went gold.

> **Tarsia:** The O'Jays had two leads and the contrast between the two vocals was terrific. Walt [Williams] had a smooth, easy tenor voice, while Eddie [Lavert] would almost inhale the mic. When I set the faders to record their vocals, I'd have to bring it way up for Walt, and almost turn it off for Eddie. I probably enjoyed recording them as much as anyone I worked with.

The O'Jays became one of the most popular vocal groups during the era of Philly soul, excelling at both love ballads and up-tempo dance tunes. Throughout the '70s, they produced nearly 30 charted singles, which included Number-1, Top-5, and Top-10 hits, such as "Backstabbers," "Love Train," "Put Your Hands Together," "I Love Music (Part I)," "Give the People What They Want," and "Use ta Be My Girl." They also recorded a series of best-selling albums. One of their classic LPs was *Ship Ahoy*, in 1973, which featured the Number-1 R&B, hit, "For the Love of Money," a stylish protest song, as well as the 10-minute title track recounting the ocean journey of African slaves.

> **Tarsia:** *Ship Ahoy* was one of the more interesting albums we did at Philly International. I felt it was an example of Kenny's personality and vision; that, underneath it all, he was always looking to deliver a message, in this case, an attempt to show what the African people went through in getting to this country. What we tried to do was emulate in caricature a slave ship. From sound effects records, I made loops of whip sounds, sailing ship rigging, and creaking noises, without any of the sophisticated digital technique we have today. I had five tape recorders running with loops on them. Kenny would hit the whips, rigging, or creaks, and we never knew what would turn up. Half of it was carefully calculated, and the rest would just fall into place. But we'd have to repeat it over and over until we got the results we wanted.

Original O'Jays member William Powell died in 1977 and was replaced by Sammy Strain, who remained with the group for 12 years. (Nathaniel Best succeeded him in 1989 and was replaced by Eric Grant in 1997.) The O'Jays continued to record through the '80s and '90s, combining their classic sound with contemporary urban R&B production. For many years, they were a consistent draw on the concert circuit, one of the most successful and long-lived vocal groups in R&B history.

Philadelphia International, which defined Philly soul, also helped to introduce disco. Beginning in the early '70s, disco music was played mostly in nightclubs (discothèques) for a dancing audience, with much of it derived from soul, funk, and salsa. The Three Degrees ("When Will I See You Again"), the Intruders ("I'll Always Love My Mama"), MFSB ("TSOP"), Evelyn "Champagne" King ("Shame"), and the Trammps all created fervor for disco in its heyday.

Founded by drummer Earl Young in the early '70s, the Trammps were a soulful group that blended two '60s bands known as the Exceptions and the Volcanos. By mid-decade, the group consisted of Jimmy Ellis (lead vocal), Harold (Doc) Wade (vocal/guitar), Stanley Wade (vocal/bass), Robert Upchurch (first tenor, who replaced earlier member Jack Hart), Ed Cermanski (keyboard), Harold Watkins (trombone), and Earl Young (drums).

Their first chart single was a spirited revival of the tune, "Zing Went the Strings of My Heart" (originally done by Judy Garland). In 1977, they had the huge hit, "Disco Inferno," written by Leroy Green and Ron Kersey (who played keyboard for the Trammps in their earlier days). The Trammps were known for their exuberant sound and jubilant harmonies.

> **Harold Watkins (the Trammps):** When we played live, Earl [Young] would let us "stretch out," take solos, and have a great interaction with the audience. Sometimes we even had low-level pyrotechnics, and there was literally fire on stage. It became almost a circus atmosphere as we brought our albums to life. There was boundless energy, and this is where we reached our pinnacle.[6]

A huge part of the group's impact came from the booming, joyful vocal quality of their lead singer Jimmy Ellis.

> **Jimmy Ellis (the Trammps):** I was able to bring an added element to the vocals because I was gospel-driven. I truly felt what I sang. I grew up singing in the church choir. What you learn singing gospel is the ability to gear up and gear

down, as some of what you sing is mournful and mellow, and at other times joyful and boisterous. The emotion and excitement that you feel lends itself to disco. What I found years later in recording sessions was the ability to ad-lib and shift gears along with the musicians' approval and encouragement. In performing live, the great joy is in connecting with my audience and making people happy. When they feel what I put out, they send it back. That heightens my performance. When they have fun, so do I. That connection is the truest form of communication, and a wonderful thing that happens in music.[7]

The Trammps maintained their popularity throughout the 1970s. In addition to their huge successes like "Disco Inferno" and "Hold Back the Night," their popular releases were "Soul Bones," "Ninety-Nine and a Half," and "I Feel Like I've Been Livin' (On the Dark Side of the Moon)."

♫ **Ed Cermanski (the Trammps):** There's evidence today of the Trammps' influence on pop culture. Artists like 50 Cent, the Game, and Mary Blige have overlaid rap lyrics to the original soundtrack of the 1971 Trammps recording of "Rubberbands" (from the legendary *Zing* album). As of August 2005, over 20 million copies have been sold.[8]

Disco music created hardships for a number of love ballad groups from the late '60s and early '70s. Many club owners stopped hiring live entertainment, because it was much cheaper to hire a D.J. to spin records and fill up their dance floors. Some recording artists were able to weather the storm by having hits in Europe. The Stylistics, for example, had a tremendous hit in England and Japan with "Can't Give You Anything But Love," reaching double platinum (for the album and the single) in both countries.

Disco faded in 1979, and the '80s brought changes for Gamble and Huff. The incredible pace of the '70s had taken their toll, and activity slowed down. In 1982, Philadelphia International's deal with Columbia expired, and they signed with EMI. That same year, fate struck a cruel blow when Teddy Pendergrass, their top recording artist, was paralyzed from injuries suffered in a near-fatal automobile accident.

Throughout the '80s and early '90s, Philadelphia International continued to produce albums sporadically for the O'Jays, Patti LaBelle, Shirley Jones, Gene McFadden and John Whitehead, the Dells, and Phyllis Hyman. In 1993, Gamble and Huff were enshrined in Philadelphia's Walk of Fame.

In recent years, Gamble has been very active in charitable causes and urban renewal, rebuilding and revitalizing the inner-city neighborhoods of Philadelphia. In 2005, Gamble and Huff were instrumental in moving the Rhythm and Blues Hall of Fame from its headquarters in New York to Philadelphia. Plans are underway to construct an R&B Hall of Fame and Philadelphia Arts and Museum Entertainment Complex, where people of all ages can come and learn about the contributions R&B and Philadelphia music have made to the world.

Recently, Philadelphia International has moved from its well-known tradition of producing artists and selling hit records to marketing the acclaimed 3500-song Gamble–Huff catalog of music, in conjunction with Warner-Chappell Music, as well as licensing the abundance of songs in its collection for commercial use around the world.

Today, amidst the oldies, classic rock, jazz, and romantic rhythm and blues played on the FM stations, new variations have evolved from '60s and '70s R&B and become part of our pop culture. Hip-hop music, which steadily grew in popularity and became mainstream during the '80s and '90s, has melded into various forms: New Jack swing, hip-hop soul, neo-soul, and, lately, an urban pop blend. However, for some contemporary artists, the era of Philly soul remains a constant influence on their work.

In late 2004, Daryl Hall and John Oates released *Our Kind of Soul*, a return to their Philly roots, with a collection of classic R&B hits from groups like the Stylistics, Spinners, O'Jays, and Teddy Pendergrass.

Kenny Gamble, Leon Huff, Thom Bell, Linda Creed, MFSB, and all the other singers, songwriters, and arrangers remembered here have left a rich legacy. Coming to us through times of civil unrest, war, and economic uncertainty, their music has offered relief, joy, solace, and inspiration.

The soulful sounds of Philadelphia have never gone away. To this day, they are revised and reinvented by new artists entering the scene. We can look back at the pop, rock, and rhythm and blues years and know that *American Bandstand,* Cameo-Parkway, and Philadelphia International Records have truly earned the City of Brotherly Love an enduring place in the musical heart of America.

42

▲ **Dick Clark,** host of *American Bandstand*, had a great rapport with the teens on his show. Together, they introduced the country to a new kind of music. In early 1963, after a successful five-and-a-half-year run in Philadelphia, *American Bandstand* moved to California and remained on the air until 1989. *Courtesy Temple University Urban Archives*

CHAPTER FIVE

The Sound of Philadelphia

By the late '60s, Kenny Gamble and Leon Huff had made steady progress on the musical horizon. They had produced a total of 10 charted songs for the Intruders (on Gamble Records) and the Soul Survivors (on Crimson), including two megahits: "Expressway to Your Heart" and "Cowboys to Girls." They also produced hits for Jerry Butler ("Only the Strong Survive," "Moody Woman," and "Hey, Western Union Man" on Mercury Records) and for Archie Bell and the Drells ("I Can't Stop Dancing" on Atlantic). In 1969, they created their second record label (Neptune) to release albums and singles through Chess.

Columbia Records took notice of their accomplishments in 1970, offering them the opportunity to create a new affiliated company, and, in early 1971, Philadelphia International Records opened their doors. With Columbia's backing (a $75,000 advance for 15 singles, and LPs budgeted at $25,000 apiece), Gamble and Huff burst onto the national scene with top hits like "Me and Mrs. Jones" by

Billy Paul, "If You Don't Know Me by Now" by Harold Melvin and the Blue Notes (also spelled Bluenotes), and "Backstabbers" and "Love Train" by the O'Jays, selling millions of records. Throughout the 1970s, Philadelphia International continued to score hits with groups like MFSB (Mother Father Sister Brother), the Three Degrees, Lou Rawls, the Jacksons, the Trammps, Teddy Pendergrass, People's Choice, and the Jones Girls (Shirley, Brenda, and Valerie).

Gamble, Huff, and Thom Bell brought a definitive sound, with full, lush orchestration. In their recording sessions, it wasn't unusual to find their ensemble composed of 18 strings, 10 horns, and a rhythm section, with added percussion, which brought the total to 40 to 50 musicians. Their combination of sweeping strings, vibrant horns, and an emphatic rhythm section embodied the Sound of Philadelphia. Their house band, MFSB, consisted of Norman Harris (guitar), Ronnie Baker (bass), Earl Young (drums), Larry Washington (percussion), Zach Zachery (sax), Vince Montana (vibes), Roland Chambers (guitar), Karl Chambers (drums), Bobby Eli (guitar), Richie Rome (piano), Leonard Pakula (keyboard), Don Renaldo (strings and horns), and, later, Ron Kersey (keyboard), T. J. Tindall (guitar), Victor Carstarphen (piano), and Dexter Wansel (keyboard). Many of the arrangements were done by Thom Bell, Bobby Martin, and, later, Jack Faith (a knowledgeable and talented musician–songwriter), who contributed heavily when Thom Bell moved to Washington.

> ♪ **Joe Tarsia:** Out of a mix of people that included Thom, Bobby, Jack Faith, Richie Rome, Roland Chambers, Lenny Pakula, Dexter Wansel, and Victor Carstarphen, Kenny found that various people had different assets. For example, Thom Bell did great strings and Bobby Martin did great horns. So, quite often we'd have two arrangers on a song. Sometimes Kenny did the arrangements. He'd call in an arranger and change things. He'd sit there and hum, and the arranger would feverishly make notes while 10 horn players waited outside. At one point, I set up a blackboard and had it painted with a staff on it. That way, the arrangers could write down the notes, and the musicians could make their changes on their charts.[1]

Philadelphia International had an interesting blend of musical creativity—both schooled musicians and musicians with feel.

> ♪ **Tarsia:** The most important element to Gamble and Huff was the feel and sincerity of the vocals and music. If they got that, and technical perfection was not there, they'd settle for 95 percent. Thom Bell, on the other side, was highly trained and extremely structured. He wrote down every note and nuance and didn't look for spontaneity. He understood every facet of his arrangements. The end result of Thom's work was a well-orchestrated, beautiful sound. Gamble and Huff looked for musicians to interpret. With Norman Harris, Ronnie Baker, and Earl Young, they could well afford that. They were adept at laying down the charts and putting their feel to the music. The riffs and figures Norman and Ronnie played weren't written down. That happened in the studio, and Earl had a relaxation and held a tempo like no drummer I have ever heard. Kenny and Leon would run down the chord chart; these guys would get into the song and feel the music. A lot of what they did was spontaneous. Then they'd take that spontaneity and run it down until they perfected the arrangement.

One of the first blockbuster hits at Philadelphia International was Billy Paul's "Me and Mrs. Jones." Paul was a unique talent, who grew up in Philadelphia and developed a vocal style that incorporated traces of jazz, R&B, and pop. His album, *Feelin' Good at the Cadillac*

▲ **Dee Dee Sharp** became a teenage idol in 1962, through her many appearances on *American Bandstand. Courtesy ABKCO*

▲ **The Dovells,** in 1961. Their memorable songs include "The Bristol Stomp," "Hully Gully Baby," and "You Can't Sit Down." *Left to right,* Arnie Silver (aka Arnie Satin), Mike Freda (aka Mike Dennis), Len Borisoff (aka Len Barry), Jerry Gross (aka Jerry Summers). *Not pictured:* Mark Gordesky (aka Mark Stevens) and Jim Mealey (aka Danny Brooks). *Courtesy ABKCO*

▲ **The Tymes,** in 1963. Shortly after they signed with Parkway Records, they record-ed "So Much in Love," which became one of the most popular ballads in music histo-ry. *Top row, left to right,* George Hilliard, Norman Burnett. *Bottom row, left to right,* Donald Banks, George Williams, Al "Caesar" Berry. *Courtesy ABKCO*

▲ **The Bluebelles,** in 1962. *Clockwise from top,* Sarah Dash, Patti LaBelle, Nona Hendryx, Cindy Birdsong. They became known as Patti LaBelle and the Bluebelles and had five charted hits within three years. In the early 1970s, they were a trio known as LaBelle. In 1977, Patti LaBelle launched a solo career. *Courtesy R&B Records*

▲ **The Cameo-Parkway Staff,** in 1964. *Standing, left to right,* Dave Appell, Bernie Lowe; *seated, left to right,* Kal Mann, Billy Jackson, and Joe Tarsia (at the console). *Courtesy Temple University Urban Archives*

▲ **Kenny Gamble,** in the late '60s. He grew up
with music in his soul and was drawn to performers with vocal distinction and character.
By the 1970s, Gamble and partner Leon Huff
were the most successful and enterprising record
producers in the country. *Photo: Weldon A.
McDougal III*

▲ **Leon Huff** began his career in music
as a gifted piano player and songwriter. He shared a great musical
chemistry with partner Kenny Gamble.
Photo: Weldon A. McDougal III

► **Solomon Burke** grew up with
gospel music. He had over 20 charted
hits in the 1960s. *Courtesy R&B
Records*

▲ **Barbara Mason,** in the '70s. In the mid- to late '60s, she became Philadelphia's "First Lady of Soul." *Photo: Weldon A. McDougal III*

▶ **The Intruders,** in 1966. *Clockwise from top,* Robert "Big Sonny" Edwards, Eugene "Bird" Daughtry, Sam "Little Sonny" Brown, and Phillip Terry. They were one of the first groups to give rise to Philly soul. *Courtesy R&B Records*

▲ **Bunny Sigler,** the grand entertainer with something for everyone. He sang songs in Hebrew, French, and Italian, in addition to pop and soul. *Photo: Weldon A. McDougal III*

▲ **Bunny Sigler,** as a teen in the early '50s. In his youth, Sigler was a gifted athlete who swam competitively against Pennsylvania's finest. On a trip to Hollywood, he raced Boy (actor Johnny Sheffield), from the Johnny Weissmuller Tarzan films, and won. When Sigler crossed the finish line, he looked back at Sheffield in honest amazement and said, "Hey, Boy, I thought you were faster than that." *Courtesy Bunny Sigler*

▲ **Tammi Terrell** teamed with Marvin Gaye to create some of the greatest love sings ever to emerge from Motown. *Courtesy Motown Records Archives*

◄ **The Soul Survivors,** in 1967. *Front to back,* Richie Ingui, Ken Jeremiah, Charlie Ingui. Their classic recording of "Expressway to Your Heart" was the first national hit for producers Kenny Gamble and Leon Huff. *Courtesy Ken Jeremiah*

▲ **Linda Creed,** the lyricist, was grand and productive. She was ultimately voted into the Songwriters Hall of Fame. *Photo: Weldon A. McDougal III*

▶ **The Stylistics,** in 1971. *Left to right,* James Smith, Herb Murrell, Russell Thompkins Jr. (lead vocal), James Dunn, and Airrion Love. With a potent and pure falsetto, Thompkins became the driving force of the group. *Courtesy Florence Thompkins*

▲ **Thom Bell** was an extraordinary arranger, who achieved great success with the Delfonics, Stylistics, and Spinners, from the late '60s through the mid-'70s. *Photo: Weldon A. McDougal III*

◄ **The Delfonics,** in 1968. *Left to right,* Randy Cain, William "Poogie" Hart, Wilbur Hart. Their unique sound influenced many R&B groups that followed. *Courtesy Temple University Urban Archives*

▲ **The O'Jays** perform "Ship Ahoy" at the Greek Theater in Los Angeles in 1973. They became one of the most successful and long-lived groups in R&B history. *Photo: Weldon A. McDougal III*

▲ **Three Degrees** (*left to right,* Valerie Holiday, Fayette Pickney, Sheila Ferguson) signed with Philadelphia International and did the vocal track for TSOP (The Sound of Philadelphia) recorded by MFSB. The song went gold and hit Number 1. That same year (1974), they recorded "When Will I See You Again," which went platinum and sold over 2 million copies. *Photo: Weldon A. McDougal III*

▲ **Billy Paul** was discovered by Charlie Parker at age 16 and worked with many jazz and R&B greats before he rose to national prominence. *Photo: Weldon A. McDougal III*

▲ Joe Jefferson, Charles Simmons, and Bruce Hawes, *left to right,* in the '70s. They became the main creative force behind the Spinners. *Photo: Weldon A. McDougal III*

▲ Harold Melvin and the Blue Notes were a great nightclub act, dazzling the audience with their showmanship. In the early to mid-'70s, they became one of the most successful groups at Philadelphia International. *Photo: Weldon A. McDougal III*

► MFSB (Mother, Father, Sister, Brother) became the house band for Philadelphia International and consisted of many highly talented and creative musicians. *Photo: Weldon A. McDougal III*

▶ **Gene McFadden,** *left,* with pianist–arranger Victor Carstarphen, *center.* McFadden became a prominent song-writer–producer at Philadelphia International during the '70s.
Photo: Weldon A. McDougal III

◀ **MFSB string section,** led by Don Renaldo.
Photo: Weldon A. McDougal III

58

▲ **John Whitehead** teamed with Gene McFadden to write and produce classic hits for the O'Jays and Harold Melvin and the Blue Notes. *Photo: Weldon A. McDougal III*

▲ **Teddy Pendergrass,** in 1980. With a surging baritone, he became one of the top R&B artists in the country. *Courtesy Temple University Urban Archives*

▲ **Joe Tarsia,** at Sigma Sound in 1973. As the chief engineer at Cameo-Parkway and, later, creator of Sigma, he recorded many great artists for over three decades. *Photo: Weldon A. McDougal III*

▲ **Weldon Arthur McDougal III,** in the mid-'70s, alongside the logo he designed for Philadelphia International Records. *Photo: Weldon A. McDougal III*

▲ **The Trammps,** in 1976. Led by the booming voice of Jimmy Ellis, they became known for their boisterous sound and jubilant harmonies. *Courtesy Ed Cermanski*

Tracks of Disc 1

1 **BUTTERFLY** ~ Charlie Gracie

2 **FABULOUS** ~ Charlie Gracie

3 **RACE FOR TIME** ~ Jerry Arnold & the Rhythm Captains

4 **SING SING SING** ~ Bernie Lowe Orchestra

5 **YOU'RE THE GREATEST** ~ Billy Scott

6 **OVER THE WEEKEND** ~ The Playboys

7 **NIGHT TIME** ~ Pete Antell

8 **MEMORY LANE** ~ The Hippies (Formerly the Tams)

9 **SILHOUETTES** ~ The Rays

10 **DADDY COOL** ~ The Rays

11 **BACK TO SCHOOL AGAIN** ~ Timmie Rogers

12 **THE CLASS** ~ Chubby Checker

13 **BAD MOTORCYCLE** ~ The Storey Sisters

14 **SHAKE A HAND** ~ Mike Pedicin Quintet

15 **DINNER WITH DRAC PART 1** ~ John Zacherle

16 **MEXICAN HAT ROCK** ~ The Applejacks

17 **NINE MORE MILES** ~ Georgie Young and the Rockin' Bocs

18 **BIRDS AND BEES** ~ The Temptations

19 **TWO WEEKS WITH PAY** ~ Georgie Young and the Rockin' Bocs

20 **ROCKA-CONGA** ~ The Applejacks

21 **KISSIN' TIME** ~ Bobby Rydell

22 **WE GOT LOVE** ~ Bobby Rydell

23 **THE TWIST** ~ Chubby Checker

24 **WILD ONE** ~ Bobby Rydell

25 **SWINGIN' SCHOOL** ~ Bobby Rydell

26 **PONY TIME** ~ Chubby Checker

27 **TEACH ME TO TWIST** ~ Chubby Checker & Bobby Rydell

28 **LET'S TWIST AGAIN** ~ Chubby Checker

29 **BRISTOL STOMP** ~ The Dovells

30 **THE WAH WATUSI** ~ The Orlons

31 **MERRY CHRISTMAS** ~ The Cameos

Tracks of Disc 2

1 **SLOW TWISTIN'** ~ Chubby Checker (With Dee Dee Sharp)

2 **MASHED POTATO TIME** ~ Dee Dee Sharp

3 **GRAVY (FOR MY MASHED POTATOES)** ~ Dee Dee Sharp

4 **DON'T HANG UP** ~ The Orlons

5 **RIDE** ~ Dee Dee Sharp

6 **DO THE NEW CONTINENTAL** ~ The Dovells

7 **THE POPEYE WADDLE** ~ Don Covay

8 **LIMBO ROCK** ~ Chubby Checker

9 **THE CHA CHA CHA** ~ Bobby Rydell

10 **VOLARE** ~ Bobby Rydell

11 **SWEET GEORGIA BROWN** ~ The Carroll Brothers

12 **BACK TO SCHOOL ONE MORE TIME**

   ~ Jerry Blavat & the Yon Teenagers

13 **(I'M THE GIRL FROM) WOLVERTON MOUNTAIN**

   ~ Jo Ann Campbell

14 **ROWDY** ~ Clint Eastwood

15 **FORGET HIM** ~ Bobby Rydell

16 **MOTHER PLEASE!** ~ Jo Ann Campbell

17 **COME ON AND DANCE WITH ME** ~ Billy Abbott and the Jewels

18 **GROOVY BABY** ~ Billy Abbott and the Jewels

19 **THE JAM PART 1** ~ Bobby Gregg and His Friends

20 **YOU CAN'T SIT DOWN** ~ The Dovells

21 **SOUTH STREET** ~ The Orlons

22 **EVERYBODY SOUTH STREET** ~ The Taffys

23 **DO THE BIRD** ~ Dee Dee Sharp

24 **NOT ME** ~ The Orlons

25 **CROSS FIRE!** ~ The Orlons

26 **(EVERYBODY DO) THE SWIM** ~ The Marlins

27 **THE 81** ~ Candy and the Kisses

28 **DAYDREAMIN' OF YOU** ~ The Dreamers

29 **THE BOY WITH THE BEATLE HAIR** ~ The Swans

30 **JINGLE BELL ROCK** ~ Chubby Checker & Bobby Rydell

Tracks of Disc 3

1 **SO MUCH IN LOVE** ~ The Tymes

2 **WONDERFUL! WONDERFUL!** ~ The Tymes

3 **I'LL BE TRUE** ~ Johnny Maestro

4 **WHEN WE GET MARRIED** ~ The Dreamlovers

5 **SOMEWHERE** ~ The Tymes

6 **HEY GOOD LOOKIN'** ~ Billy Abbott and the Jewels

7 **JUST ONE CHANCE** ~ The Sparkletones

8 **YOU'LL NEVER WALK ALONE** ~ Patti LaBelle and the Bluebelles

9 **DANNY BOY** ~ Patti LaBelle and the Bluebelles

10 **CAST YOUR FATE TO THE WIND** ~ Sounds Orchestral

11 **IT ONLY TOOK A MINUTE** ~ Joe Brown and the Bruvvers

12 **LONG TALL SALLY** ~ The Kinks

13 **BOYS** ~ Peter Best

14 **YOU STILL WANT ME** ~ The Kinks

15 **FUNNY HOW LOVE CAN BE** ~ The Ivy League

16 **TOSSING & TURNING** ~ The Ivy League

17 **SHE'S FALLEN IN LOVE WITH THE MONSTER MAN**
~ Screamin' Lord Sutch & the Savages

18 **WILD THING** ~ Senator Bobby

19 **LITTLE WHITE HOUSE** ~ Len Barry

20 **FOOL, FOOL, FOOL** ~ Joey and the Flips

21 **GIRL FROM NEW YORK CITY** ~ The GTOs

22 **SOCIETY GIRL** ~ The Rag Dolls

23 **SOLDIER BABY OF MINE** ~ Candy and the Kisses

24 **S.O.S. (HEART IN DISTRESS)** ~ Christine Cooper

25 **BECAUSE OF MY HEART** ~ Frankie Beverly and the Butlers

26 **HEARTACHES AWAY MY BOY** ~ Christine Cooper

27 **GOT TO RUN** ~ Vickie Baines

28 **MY BOY** ~ The Stylettes

29 **WHITE CHRISTMAS (3 O'CLOCK WEATHER REPORT)**
~ Bobby the Poet

Tracks of Disc 4

1 **ANGEL OF THE MORNING** ~ Evie Sands

2 **THE LOVE OF A BOY** ~ Evie Sands

3 **THIS CAN'T BE TRUE** ~ Eddie Holman

4 **WORLD OF FANTASY** ~ The Five Stairsteps

5 **COME BACK** ~ The Five Stairsteps

6 **AM I A LOSER** ~ Eddie Holman

7 **DANGER! SHE'S A STRANGER** ~ The Five Stairsteps

8 **MEET ME IN CHURCH** ~ Bobby Marchan

9 **YOU'VE BEEN UNTRUE** ~ The Delfonics

10 **GET A HOLD OF YOURSELF** ~ The Persians

11 **HE DON'T REALLY LOVE YOU** ~ The Delfonics

12 **THE SWEETEST THING THIS SIDE OF HEAVEN** ~ Chris Bartley

13 **THE GRASS WILL SING FOR YOU** ~ Lonnie Youngblood

14 **I (WHO HAVE NOTHING)** ~ Terry Knight and the Pack

15 **BEG, BORROW AND STEAL** ~ Ohio Express

16 **96 TEARS** ~ ? & the Mysterians

17 **I NEED SOMEBODY** ~ ? & the Mysterians

18 **EAST SIDE STORY** ~ Bob Seger

19 **CAN'T GET ENOUGH OF YOU, BABY** ~ ? & the Mysterians

20 **RESPECT** ~ The Rationals

21 **SHAKE YOUR TAMBOURINE** ~ Bobby Marchan

22 **LET THE GOOD TIMES ROLL & FEELS SO GOOD** ~ Bunny Sigler

23 **HEAVY MUSIC PART 1** ~ Bob Seger and the Last Heard

24 **LOVEY DOVEY / YOU'RE SO FINE** ~ Bunny Sigler

25 **SOCK IT TO ME SANTA** ~ Bob Seger and the Last Heard

CAMEO-PARKWAY INDIVIDUAL ARTIST ALBUMS

Released by ABKCO Music and Records 2005

THE BEST OF BOBBY RYDELL

1   PLEASE DON'T BE MAD
2   ALL I WANT IS YOU
3   WE GOT LOVE
4   KISSIN' TIME
5   I DIG GIRLS
6   WILD ONE
7   DING-A-LING
8   SWINGIN' SCHOOL
9   LITTLE BITTY GIRL
10 VOLARE
11 SWAY
12 THAT OLD BLACK MAGIC
13 I WANNA THANK YOU
14 BUTTERFLY BABY
15 GOOD TIME BABY
16 I'VE GOT BONNIE
17 I'LL NEVER DANCE AGAIN
18 THE THIRD HOUSE
19 WILDWOOD DAYS
20 THE CHA-CHA-CHA
21 THE BEST MAN CRIED
22 FORGET HIM
23 A WORLD WITHOUT LOVE
24 JINGLE BELL ROCK
25 A MESSAGE FROM BOBBY

THE BEST OF CHUBBY CHECKER

1   DANCIN' PARTY
2   THE TWIST
3   TOOT
4   THE CLASS
5   TWISTIN' USA
6   THE HUCKLEBUCK
7   WHOLE LOTTA SHAKIN' GOING ON
8   PONY TIME
9   DANCE THE MESS AROUND
10 GOOD, GOOD LOVIN'
11 LET'S TWIST AGAIN
12 THE FLY
13 SLOW TWISTIN'
14 POPEYE THE HITCHHIKER
15 LIMBO ROCK
16 LET'S LIMBO SOME MORE
17 HOOKA TOOKA
18 LODDY LO
19 HEY, BOBBA NEEDLE
20 BIRDLAND
21 SURF PARTY
22 TWIST IT UP
23 TWISTIN' ROUND THE WORLD
24 JINGLE BELL ROCK

THE BEST OF DEE DEE SHARP

1 MASHED POTATO TIME
2 GRAVY (FOR MY MASHED POTATOES)
3 BABY CAKES
4 YOU ARE MY SUNSHINE
5 RIDE!
6 DO THE BIRD
7 SLOW TWISTIN'
8 YOU AIN'T NOTHIN' BUT A NOTHIN'
9 JUST TO HOLD MY HAND
10 ROCK ME IN THE CRADLE OF LOVE
11 WILD!
12 WHY DONCHA ASK ME
13 NEVER PICK A PRETTY BOY
14 WILLYAM, WILLYAM
15 WHERE DID I GO WRONG
16 DEEP DARK SECRET
17 THERE AIN'T NOTHIN' I WOULDN'T DO FOR YOU
18 (THAT'S WHAT) MY MAMA SAID
19 LET'S TWINE
20 STANDING IN THE NEED OF LOVE
21 IT'S A FUNNY SITUATION
22 I REALLY LOVE YOU
23 (IT'S WONDERFUL) THE LOVE I FEEL FOR YOU
24 TO KNOW HIM IS TO LOVE HIM

THE BEST OF THE DOVELLS

1 BRISTOL STOMP
2 NO, NO, NO
3 FOOT STOMPIN'
4 MOPE-ITTY MOPE
5 DO THE NEW CONTINENTAL
6 THE ACTOR
7 BRISTOL TWISTIN' ANNIE
8 HULLY GULLY BABY
9 YOUR LAST CHANCE
10 KISSIN' IN THE KITCHEN
11 THE JITTERBUG
12 YOU CAN'T SIT DOWN
13 BABY WORKOUT
14 HEY BEAUTIFUL
15 BETTY IN BERMUDAS
16 DANCE THE FROOG
17 STOP MONKEYIN' AROUND
18 DON'T COME BACK
19 LITTLE WHITE HOUSE
20 HEARTS ARE TRUMP
21 1-2-3

THE BEST OF THE ORLONS

1 I'LL BE TRUE
2 THE WAH-WATUSI
3 DON'T HANG UP
4 THE CONSERVATIVE
5 SOUTH STREET
6 CEMENT MIXER
7 NOT ME
8 CROSSFIRE!
9 DON'T THROW YOUR LOVE AWAY
10 BON-DOO-WAH
11 EVERYTHING NICE
12 SHIMMY, SHIMMY
13 RULES OF LOVE
14 HEARTBREAK HOTEL
15 KNOCK, KNOCK (WHO'S THERE?)
16 GOIN' PLACES
17 ENVY (IN MY EYES)
18 DON'T YOU WANT MY LOVIN'
19 SPINNING TOP
20 MR. TWENTY-ONE

THE BEST OF THE TYMES

1 SO MUCH IN LOVE
2 WONDERFUL! WONDERFUL!
3 COME WITH ME TO THE SEA
4 STRANGER IN PARADISE
5 MALIBU
6 WORDS WRITTEN ON WATER
7 ANYMORE
8 SOMEWHERE
9 HERE SHE COMES
10 HELLO YOUNG LOVERS
11 WAY BEYOND TODAY
12 ONE LITTLE KISS
13 ADDRESS UNKNOWN
14 WONDERLAND OF LOVE
15 TO EACH HIS OWN
16 CHANCES ARE
17 MY SUMMER LOVE
18 THE MAGIC OF OUR SUMMER LOVE
19 THE LAMP IS LOW
20 AND THAT REMINDS ME
21 VIEW FROM MY WINDOW
22 GOODNIGHT MY LOVE

POP AND R&B CHART SONGS
1965–1991

Released on Philadelphia International, Gamble Records, Neptune Records, TSOP, Golden Fleece, and other associated labels

By
Kenny Gamble • Leon Huff • Thom Bell • Linda Creed • Jerry Butler • Bunny Sigler • Cary Gilbert • Gene McFadden • John Whitehead • Joseph Jefferson • Bruce Hawes • Charles Simmons • Phil Hurtt • Norman Harris • Allan Felder • Sherman Marshall • Ted Wortham • Ronnie Baker • Bobby Eli • Cynthia Biggs • Victor Carstarphen • Dexter Wansel • Talmadge Conway • Weldon McDougal III • Joe Simon • Phil Terry • Theodore Life • James Bishop • Charles Ingui • Richard Ingui • Eddie Lavert • Russell Thompkins • and other associated artists

From
Gamble-Huff Music/Warner-Chappell Music Ltd.

1965

I REALLY LOVE YOU
(Kenny Gamble/James Bishop)
Dee Dee Sharp (Cameo)

1966

I'M GONNA MAKE YOU LOVE ME
(Kenny Gamble/Leon Huff/Jerry Ross)
Dee Dee Warwick (Mercury)

UNITED
(Kenny Gamble/Leon Huff)
The Intruders (Gamble)
Peaches & Herb (Date)

1967

BABY I'M LONELY TONIGHT
(Kenny Gamble/Leon Huff)
The Intruders (Gamble)

EXPRESSWAY TO YOUR HEART
(Kenny Gamble/Leon Huff)
Soul Survivors (Crimson)

A LOVE THAT'S REAL
(Kenny Gamble/Leon Huff)
The Intruders (Gamble)

TOGETHER
(Kenny Gamble/Leon Huff)
The Intruders (Gamble)

1968

CHECK YOURSELF
(Kenny Gamble/Leon Huff)
Italian Asphalt & Pavement Company (Colossus)

COWBOYS TO GIRLS
(Kenny Gamble/Leon Huff)
The Intruders (Gamble)

DO THE CHOO CHOO
(Kenny Gamble/Leon Huff)
Archie Bell and the Drells (Atlantic)

EXPLOSION IN MY SOUL
(Kenny Gamble/Leon Huff)
Soul Survivors (Crimson)

HEY WESTERN UNION MAN
(Kenny Gamble/Leon Huff/Jerry Butler)
Jerry Butler (Mercury)

I CAN'T STOP DANCING
(Kenny Gamble/Leon Huff)
Archie Bell and the Drells (Atlantic)

I'M GONNA MAKE YOU LOVE ME
(Kenny Gamble/Leon Huff/Jerry Ross)
Madeline Bell (Philips)

I'M SORRY
(Thom Bell/William Hart)
The Delfonics (Philly Groove)

IMPOSSIBLE MISSION
(Kenny Gamble/Leon Huff)
Soul Survivors (Crimson)

LA LA MEANS I LOVE YOU
(Thom Bell/William Hart)
The Delfonics (Philly Groove)

LET'S MAKE A PROMISE
(Kenny Gamble/Mikki Farrow/Thom Bell)
Peaches & Herb (Date)

LOST
(Kenny Gamble/Leon Huff/Jerry Butler)
Jerry Butler (Mercury)

LOVE IN THEM THERE HILLS
(Kenny Gamble/Leon Huff/Roland Chambers)
The Vibrations (Okeh)

(LOVE IS LIKE A) BASEBALL GAME
(Kenny Gamble/Leon Huff)
The Intruders (Gamble)

NEVER GONNA GIVE YOU UP
(Kenny Gamble/Leon Huff/Jerry Butler)
Jerry Butler (Mercury)

ONLY THE STRONG SURVIVE
(Kenny Gamble/Leon Huff/Jerry Butler)
Jerry Butler (Mercury)

SLOW DRAG
(Kenny Gamble/Leon Huff)
The Intruders (Gamble)

UNITED
(Kenny Gamble/Leon Huff)
Music Makers (Gamble)

1969

ARE YOU HAPPY
(Kenny Gamble/Theresa Bell/Jerry Butler)
Jerry Butler (Mercury)

BRAND NEW ME
(Kenny Gamble/Theresa Bell/Jerry Butler)
Dusty Springfield (Atlantic)

DON'T LET LOVE HANG YOU UP
(Kenny Gamble/Leon Huff/Jerry Butler)
Jerry Butler (Mercury)

GIRL YOU'RE TOO YOUNG
(Kenny Gamble/Thom Bell/Archie Bell)
Archie Bell and the Drells (Atlantic)

I LOVE MY BABY
(Kenny Gamble/Theresa Bell)
Archie Bell and the Drells (Atlantic)

I'M GONNA MAKE YOU LOVE ME
(Kenny Gamble/Leon Huff/Jerry Ross)
**Diana Ross and the Supremes/
The Temptations** (Motown)

MOODY WOMAN
(Kenny Gamble/Theresa Bell/Jerry Butler)
Jerry Butler (Mercury)

MY BALLOON'S GOING UP
(Kenny Gamble/Leon Huff)
Archie Bell and the Drells
(Atlantic)

OLD LOVE (LET'S START ALL OVER)
(Kenny Gamble/Leon Huff)
The Intruders (Gamble)

ONE NIGHT AFFAIR
(Kenny Gamble/Leon Huff)
The O'Jays (Neptune)

ONLY THE STRONG SURVIVE
(Kenny Gamble/Leon Huff/Jerry Butler)
Jerry Butler (Mercury)

**READY OR NOT HERE I COME
(CAN'T HIDE FROM LOVE)**
(Thom Bell/William Hart)
The Delfonics (Philly Groove)

SOMEBODY LOVES YOU
(Thom Bell/William Hart)
The Delfonics (Philly Groove)

THERE'S GONNA BE A SHOWDOWN
(Kenny Gamble/Leon Huff)
Archie Bell and the Drells
(Atlantic)

WHAT'S THE USE OF BREAKING UP
(Kenny Gamble/Theresa Bell/Jerry Butler)
Jerry Butler (Mercury)

1970

(GOTTA FIND) A BRAND NEW LOVER
(Kenny Gamble/Leon Huff)
The Sweet Inspirations (Atlantic)

BRAND NEW ME
(Kenny Gamble/Theresa Bell/Jerry Butler)
Aretha Franklin (Atlantic)

DEEPER (IN LOVE WITH YOU)
(Kenny Gamble/Leon Huff)
The O'Jays (Neptune)

DIDN'T I (BLOW YOUR MIND THIS TIME)
(Thom Bell/William Hart)
The Delfonics (Philly Groove)

GET ME BACK ON TIME ENGINE NUMBER 9
(Kenny Gamble/Leon Huff)
Wilson Pickett (Atlantic)

I COULD WRITE A BOOK (ABOUT THE WAY YOU HURT ME)
(Kenny Gamble/Leon Huff/Jerry Butler)
Jerry Butler (Mercury)

THIS IS MY LOVE SONG
(Kenny Gamble/Leon Huff)
The Intruders (Gamble)

TRYING TO MAKE A FOOL OF ME
(Thom Bell/William Hart)
The Delfonics (Philly Groove)

WORLD WITHOUT MUSIC
(Kenny Gamble/Leon Huff)
Archie Bell and the Drells (Atlantic)

1971

DETERMINATION
(Kenny Gamble/Leon Huff)
The Ebonys (Phil. Int.)

DON'T LET THE GREEN GRASS FOOL YOU
(Jerry Akines/Johnnie Bellmon/
Victor Drayton/Reginald Turner)
Wilson Pickett (Atlantic)

HELP ME FIND A WAY (TO SAY I LOVE YOU)
(Thom Bell/Linda Creed)
Little Anthony and the Imperials (United Artists)

I BET HE DON'T LOVE YOU
(Kenny Gamble/Leon Huff)
The Intruders (Gamble)

I'M GIRL SCOUTIN'
(Kenny Gamble/Leon Huff)
The Intruders (Gamble)

NOW I'M A WOMAN
(Kenny Gamble/Leon Huff)
Nancy Wilson (Capitol)

PRAY FOR ME
(Kenny Gamble/Leon Huff)
The Intruders (Gamble)

STOP LOOK LISTEN (TO YOUR HEART)
(Thom Bell/Linda Creed)
The Stylistics (AVCO Embassy)

YOU'RE THE REASON WHY
(Kenny Gamble/Leon Huff)
The Ebonys (Phil. Int.)

1972

992 ARGUMENTS
(Kenny Gamble/Leon Huff)
The O'Jays (Phil. Int.)

BACK STABBERS
(Leon Huff/Gene McFadden/John
Whitehead)
The O'Jays (Phil. Int.)

BETCHA BY GOLLY WOW
(Thom Bell/Linda Creed)
The Stylistics (AVCO)

DROWNING IN THE SEA OF LOVE
(Kenny Gamble/Leon Huff)
Joe Simon (Spring)

HOW COULD I LET YOU GET AWAY
(Yvette Davis)
The Spinners (Atlantic)

I FOUND MY DAD
(Bunny Sigler/Phil Hurtt)
Joe Simon (Spring)

I MISS YOU (PARTS 1 & 2)
(Kenny Gamble/Leon Huff)
Harold Melvin and the Blue Notes (Phil.
Int.)

I'LL BE AROUND
(Thom Bell/Phil Hurtt)
The Spinners (Atlantic)

I'M STONE IN LOVE WITH YOU
(Thom Bell/Linda Creed/Anthony Bell)
The Stylistics (AVCO)

IF YOU DON'T KNOW ME BY NOW
(Kenny Gamble/Leon Huff)
Harold Melvin and the Blue Notes (Phil.
Int.)

ME AND MRS. JONES
(Kenny Gamble/Leon Huff/Cary Gilbert)
Billy Paul (Phil. Int.)

ONE NIGHT AFFAIR
(Kenny Gamble/Leon Huff)
Jerry Butler (Mercury)

**PEOPLE MAKE THE WORLD GO
ROUND**
(Thom Bell/Linda Creed)
The Stylistics (AVCO)

POOL OF BAD LUCK
(Kenny Gamble/Leon Huff)
Joe Simon (Spring)

POWER OF LOVE
(Kenny Gamble/Leon Huff/Joe Simon)
Joe Simon (Spring)

**(WIN PLACE OR SHOW)
SHE'S A WINNER**
(Kenny Gamble/Leon Huff)
The Intruders (Gamble)

SLOW MOTION
(Kenny Gamble/Leon Huff)
Johnny Williams (Phil. Int.)

YOU ARE EVERYTHING
(Thom Bell/Linda Creed)
The Stylistics (AVCO)

1973

AM I BLACK ENOUGH FOR YOU
(Kenny Gamble/Leon Huff)
Billy Paul (Phil. Int.)

**ARMED AND EXTREMELY
DANGEROUS**
(Norman Harris/Allan Felder)
First Choice (Philly Groove)

BREAK UP TO MAKE UP
(Thom Bell/Linda Creed/Kenny Gamble)
The Stylistics (AVCO)

COULD IT BE I'M FALLING IN LOVE
(Melvin Steals/Mervin Steals)
The Spinners (Atlantic)

DIRTY OL' MAN
(Kenny Gamble/Leon Huff)
Three Degrees (Phil. Int.)

GHETTO CHILD
(Thom Bell/Linda Creed)
The Spinners (Atlantic)

I WANNA KNOW YOUR NAME
(Kenny Gamble/Leon Huff)
The Intruders (Gamble)

I'LL ALWAYS LOVE MY MAMA
(Kenny Gamble/Leon Huff/
Gene McFadden/John Whitehead)
The Intruders (Gamble)

I'M A WINNER NOW
(Allan Felder/Norman Harris)
Executive Suite (Babylon)

I'M COMING HOME
(Thom Bell/Linda Creed)
Johnny Mathis (Columbia)

I'M DOIN' FINE NOW
(Thom Bell/Sherman Marshall)
New York City (Chelsea)

INTERNATIONAL PLAYBOY
(Eugene Dozier/Bunny Sigler/
Bernard Broomer/Lee Philips)
Wilson Pickett (Atlantic)

IT'S FOREVER
(Leon Huff)
The Ebonys (Phil. Int.)

JUST CAN'T GET YOU OUT OF MY MIND
(Vinnie Barrett)
Baby Washington (Master)

JUST DON'T WANT TO BE LONELY
(Vinnie Barrett/Bobby Eli/John Freeman)
Ronnie Dyson (Columbia)

THE LOVE I LOST
(Kenny Gamble/Leon Huff)
Harold Melvin and the Blue Notes (Phil. Int.)

LOVE TRAIN
(Kenny Gamble/Leon Huff)
The O'Jays (Phil. Int.)

ONE MAN BAND (PLAYS ALL ALONE)
(Thom Bell/Linda Creed)
Ronnie Dyson (Columbia)

ONE OF A KIND (LOVE AFFAIR)
(Joseph Jefferson)
The Spinners (Atlantic)

ROCKIN' ROLL BABY
(Thom Bell/Linda Creed)
The Stylistics (AVCO)

SUNSHINE
(Bunny Sigler/Phil Hurtt)
Percy Sledge (Atlantic)

SWEET CHARLIE BABE
(Bunny Sigler/Phil Hurtt)
Jackie Moore (Atlantic)

TIME TO GET DOWN
(Kenny Gamble/Leon Huff)
The O'Jays (Phil. Int.)

YESTERDAY I HAD THE BLUES
(Kenny Gamble/Leon Huff)
Harold Melvin and the Blue Notes (Phil. Int.)

1974

BE TRUTHFUL TO ME
(Kenny Gamble/Leon Huff/
Gene McFadden/John Whitehead)
Billy Paul (Phil. Int.)

BINGO
(Norman Harris/Bunny Sigler/
Allan Felder)
The Whispers (Janus)

CITY OF BROTHERLY LOVE
(Richard Ingui/Charles Ingui)
Soul Survivors (TSOP)

FOR THE LOVE OF MONEY
(Kenny Gamble/Leon Huff/
Anthony Jackson)
The O'Jays (Phil. Int.)

GOOD THINGS DON'T LAST FOREVER
(Norman Harris/Bunny Sigler/
Allan Felder)
Ecstasy, Passion & Pain (Roulette)

HAPPINESS IS
(Charles Simmons/Joseph Jefferson/
Bruce Hawes)
New York City (Chelsea)

I'M COMING HOME
(Thom Bell/Linda Creed)
The Spinners (Atlantic)

I'M FALLING IN LOVE WITH YOU
(Jean Davis)
Little Anthony and the Imperials
(AVCO)

I'M WEAK FOR YOU
(Kenny Gamble/Leon Huff/Cary Gilbert)
Harold Melvin and the Blue Notes (Phil.
Int.)

JUST DON'T WANT TO BE LONELY
(Vinnie Barrett/Bobby Eli/John Freeman)
The Main Ingredient (RCA)

KEEP SMILIN'
(Allan Felder/Bunny Sigler)
Bunny Sigler (Phil. Int.)

LIFE IN THE COUNTRY
(Theodore Life/Talmadge Conway/
Phillip Terry)
The Ebonys (Phil. Int.)

LIFE IS A SONG WORTH SINGING
(Thom Bell/Linda Creed)
Johnny Mathis (Columbia)

LOVE DON'T LOVE NOBODY
(Joseph Jefferson/Charles Simmons)
The Spinners (Atlantic)

LOVE EPIDEMIC
(Norman Harris/LeRoy Green)
The Trammps (Golden Fleece)

LOVE IS THE MESSAGE
(Kenny Gamble/Leon Huff)
MFSB featuring the Three Degrees (Phil.
Int.)

LOVE TRAIN
(Kenny Gamble/Leon Huff)
Bunny Sigler (Phil. Int.)

MIGHTY LOVE
(Bruce Hawes, Joseph Jefferson/
Charles Simmons)
The Spinners (Atlantic)

A MOTHER FOR MY CHILDREN
(Norman Harris/Bunny Sigler/ Allan
Felder/Ronnie Baker)
The Whispers (Janus)

A NICE GIRL LIKE YOU
(Kenny Gamble/Leon Huff)
The Intruders (TSOP)

THE PLAYER
(Allan Felder/Norman Harris)
First Choice (Philly Groove)

POWER OF LOVE
(Kenny Gamble/Leon Huff/
Joe Simon)
Martha Reeves (MCA)

PUT YOUR HANDS TOGETHER
(Kenny Gamble/Leon Huff)
The O'Jays (Phil. Int.)

QUICK FAST IN A HURRY
(Thom Bell/Linda Creed)
New York City (Chelsea)

**SATISFACTION GUARANTEED
(OR TAKE YOUR LOVE BACK)**
(Kenny Gamble/Leon Huff)
Harold Melvin and the Blue Notes (Phil. Int.)

SIDESHOW
(Vinnie Barrett/Bobby Eli)
Blue Magic (ATCO)

THANKS FOR SAVING MY LIFE
(Kenny Gamble/Leon Huff)
Billy Paul (Phil. Int.)

THEN CAME YOU
(Phillip Pugh/Sherman Marshall)
**Dionne Warwick/
The Spinners** (Atlantic)

THREE RING CIRCUS
(Bobby Eli/Vinnie Barrett)
Blue Magic (ATCO)

TRUSTING HEART
(Mervin Steals/Melvin Steals)
The Trammps (Golden Fleece)

**TSOP
(THE SOUND OF PHILADELPHIA)**
(Kenny Gamble/Leon Huff)
MFSB featuring the Three Degrees (Phil. Int.)

WHAT MORE CAN A GIRL ASK FOR
(Norman Harris/Allan Felder)
The Whispers (Janus)

WHEN WILL I SEE YOU AGAIN
(Kenny Gamble/Leon Huff)
The Three Degrees (Phil. Int.)

WHERE ARE ALL MY FRIENDS
(Victor Carstarphen/Gene McFadden/John Whitehead)
Harold Melvin and the Blue Notes (Phil. Int.)

WHERE DO WE GO FROM HERE
(Ronnie Baker)
The Trammps (Golden Fleece)

YEAR OF DECISION
(Kenny Gamble/Leon Huff)
The Three Degrees (Phil. Int.)

YOU BRING OUT THE BEST IN ME
(Thom Bell/Linda Creed)
Derek & Cyndi (Thunder)

YOU MAKE ME FEEL BRAND NEW
(Thom Bell/Linda Creed)
The Stylistics (AVCO)

1975

BAD LUCK
(Gene McFadden/John Whitehead/Victor Carstarphen)
Harold Melvin and the Blue Notes (Phil. Int.)

BILLY'S BACK HOME
(Dexter Wansel)
Billy Paul (Phil. Int.)

DO IT ANY WAY YOU WANNA
(Leon Huff)
People's Choice (TSOP)

DON'T TAKE YOUR LOVE FROM ME
(Bunny Sigler/Allan Felder)
The Manhattans (Columbia)

EXPRESSWAY TO YOUR HEART
(Kenny Gamble/Leon Huff)
Margo Thunder (Haven)

FREE MAN
(Ronnie Tyson/Bunny Sigler)
South Shore Commission (Wand)

GIVE THE PEOPLE WHAT THEY WANT
(Kenny Gamble/Leon Huff)
The O'Jays (Phil. Int.)

HOOKED FOR LIFE
(Allan Felder/Norman Harris/
Bunny Sigler)
The Trammps (Atlantic)

**HOPE THAT WE CAN BE TOGETHER
SOON**
(Kenny Gamble/Leon Huff)
**Sharon Paige with Harold Melvin and the
Blue Notes** (Phil. Int.)

I COULD DANCE ALL NIGHT
(Ronnie Tyson/Bunny Sigler/
Allan Felder)
Archie Bell and the Drells (TSOP)

I DIDN'T KNOW
(Jean Lang/Bunny Sigler)
The Three Degrees (Phil. Int.)

I LOVE MUSIC
(Kenny Gamble/Leon Huff)
The O'Jays (Phil. Int.)

IF YOU DON'T NOW ME BY NOW
(Kenny Gamble/Leon Huff)
Lyn Collins (People)

LET ME MAKE LOVE TO YOU
(Allan Felder/Bunny Sigler)
The O'Jays (Phil. Int.)

LIVING A LITTLE LAUGHING A LITTLE
(Thom Bell/Linda Creed)
The Spinners (Atlantic)

LOVE IS WHAT YOU MAKE IT
(Bruce Hawes/ Joseph Jefferson/
Charles Simmons)
New York City (Chelsea)

LOVE WON'T LET ME WAIT
(Vinnie Barrett/Bobby Eli)
Major Harris (Atlantic)

ME AND MRS. JONES
(Kenny Gamble/Leon Huff/
Cary Gilbert)
Ron Banks and the Dramatics (ABC)

SADIE
(Bruce Hawes/Joseph Jefferson/
Charles Simmons)
The Spinners (Atlantic)

SEXY
(Kenny Gamble/Leon Huff)
MFSB (Phil. Int.)

SUNSHINE
(Bunny Sigler/Phil Hurtt)
The O'Jays (Phil. Int.)

SURVIVAL
(Kenny Gamble/Leon Huff)
The O'Jays (Phil. Int.)

**T.L.C.
(TENDER LOVIN' CARE)**
(Robert Martin/Norman Harris)
MFSB (Phil. Int.)

**THEY JUST CAN'T STOP IT
(GAMES PEOPLE PLAY)**
(Bruce Hawes/Joseph Jefferson/
Charles Simmons)
The Spinners (Atlantic)

WHAT CAN I DO FOR YOU
(Charles Simmons/Joseph Jefferson/
Richard Roebuck)
Patti LaBelle (Epic)

YOU'RE AS RIGHT AS RAIN
(Thom Bell/Linda Creed)
Nancy Wilson (Capitol)

THE ZIP
(Kenny Gamble/Leon Huff)
MFSB (Phil. Int.)

1976

BAD LUCK
(Gene McFadden/John Whitehead/
Victor Carstarphen)
Atlanta Disco Band (Ariola)

BE FOR REAL
(Leon Huff/Cary Gilbert)
Marlena Shaw (Blue Notes)

ENJOY YOURSELF
(Kenny Gamble/Leon Huff)
The Jacksons (Epic)

**EVERYMAN
(HAS TO CARRY HIS OWN WEIGHT)**
(Allan Felder/Bunny Sigler)
Double Exposure (Salsoul)

FAMILY REUNION
(Kenny Gamble/Leon Huff)
The O'Jays (Phil. Int.)

GROOVY PEOPLE
(Kenny Gamble/Leon Huff)
Lou Rawls (Phil. Int.)

HE'S A FRIEND
(Allan Felder/Bruce Gray/
Talmadge Conway)
Eddie Kendricks (Tamla)

HERE WE GO AGAIN
(Leon Huff)
People's Choice (TSOP)

HIS HOUSE AND ME
(Thom Bell/Linda Creed)
Dionne Warwick (Warner Bros.)

KEEP SMILIN'
(Allan Felder/Bunny Sigler)
Gabor Szabo (Mercury)

L.A. SUNSHINE
(Michael Burton/Phillip Terry)
Sylvia (Vibration)

LET'S GROOVE
(Gene McFadden/John Whitehead/
Victor Carstarphen/Leon Huff)
Archie Bell and the Drells (TSOP)

LET'S MAKE A BABY
(Kenny Gamble/Leon Huff)
Billy Paul (Phil. Int.)

LIFE ON MARS (PART 1)
(Dexter Wansel)
Dexter Wansel (Phil. Int.)

LIVIN' FOR THE WEEKEND
(Kenny Gamble/Leon Huff/
Cary Gilbert)
The O'Jays (Phil. Int.)

LOVE OR LEAVE
(Bruce Hawes/Joseph Jefferson/
Charles Simmons)
The Spinners (Atlantic)

MESSAGE IN OUR MUSIC
(Kenny Gamble/Leon Huff)
The O'Jays (Phil. Int.)

MOVIN' IN ALL DIRECTIONS
(Leon Huff/Darnell Jordan/
Donald Ford)
People's Choice (TSOP)

MY MUSIC
(Bunny Sigler, Leon Huff/John Whitehead/
Gene McFadden/Victor Carstarphen)
Bunny Sigler (Phil. Int.)

NURSERY RHYMES
(Leon Huff/Cary Gilbert)
People's Choice (TSOP)

ONCE YOU HIT THE ROAD
(Charles Simmons/Joseph Jefferson)
Dionne Warwick (Warner Bros.)

PEOPLE POWER
(Gene McFadden/John Whitehead/
Victor Carstarphen)
Billy Paul (Phil. Int.)

THE RUBBERBAND MAN
(Thom Bell/Linda Creed)
The Spinners (Atlantic)

THE SOUL CITY WALK
(Gene McFadden/John Whitehead/
Victor Carstarphen)
Archie Bell and the Drells (TSOP)

STAIRWAY TO HEAVEN
(Kenny Gamble/Leon Huff)
The O'Jays (Phil. Int.)

**SUMMERTIME AND I'M FEELIN'
MELLOW**
(Victor Carstarphen/Gene McFadden/
John Whitehead)
MFSB (Phil. Int.)

SUNSHINE
(Bunny Sigler/Phil Hurtt)
The Impressions (Curtom)

**TELL THE WORLD HOW I FEEL ABOUT
'CHA**
(Gene McFadden/John Whitehead/
Victor Carstarphen)
Harold Melvin and the Blue Notes (Phil. Int.)

TEN PERCENT
(Allan Felder/Talmadge Conway)
Double Exposure (Salsoul)

TOUCH AND GO
(Allan Felder/Norman Harris/Bunny Sigler)
Ecstasy, Passion & Pain (Roulette)

TRAIN CALLED FREEDOM
(Bunny Sigler/Ronnie Tyson)
South Shore Commission (Wand)

WAKE UP EVERYBODY
(Gene McFadden/John Whitehead/
Victor Carstarphen)
Harold Melvin and the Blue Notes (Phil. Int.)

WAKE UP SUSAN
(Sherman Marshall/Thom Bell)
The Spinners (Atlantic)

**YOU'LL NEVER FIND ANOTHER LOVE
LIKE MINE**
(Kenny Gamble/Leon Huff)
Lou Rawls (Phil. Int.)

1977

**AFTER YOU LOVE ME
WHY DO YOU LEAVE ME**
(Kenny Gamble/Harold Melvin/Bruce Hawes)
**Harold Melvin and the Blue Notes
featuring Sharon Paige** (ABC)

BETCHA BY GOLLY WOW
(Thom Bell/Linda Creed)
**Norman Connors featuring
Phyllis Hyman** (Buddah)

**COLD BLOODED AND
DOWN-RIGHT-FUNKY**
(Leon Huff/Frankie Brunson)
People's Choice (TSOP)

**DARLIN' DARLIN' BABY
(SWEET TENDER LOVE)**
(Kenny Gamble/Leon Huff)
The O'Jays (Phil. Int.)

DON'T LEAVE ME THIS WAY
(Kenny Gamble/Leon Huff/
Cary Gilbert)
Thelma Houston (Tamla)

EVERYBODY HAVE A GOOD TIME
(Bunny Sigler)
Archie Bell and the Drells
(Phil. Int.)

FREE LOVE
(Kenny Gamble/Leon Huff)
Jean Carn (Phil. Int.)

GLAD YOU COULD MAKE IT
(Victor Carstarphen)
Archie Bell and the Drells
(Phil. Int.)

GOIN' PLACES
(Kenny Gamble/Leon Huff)
The Jacksons (Epic)

HEAVEN ON EARTH (SO FINE)
(Casey James)
The Spinners (Atlantic)

HOW GOOD IS YOUR GAME
(Michael Burton/Phillip Terry)
Billy Paul (Phil. Int.)

I DON'T LOVE YOU ANYMORE
(Kenny Gamble/Leon Huff)
Teddy Pendergrass (Phil. Int.)

**I GOT A NOTION
(YOU GOT THE MOTION)**
(Philippe Wynne)
Al Hudson & the Soul Partners (ABC)

I TRUST YOU
(Kenny Gamble/Leon Huff)
Billy Paul (Phil. Int.)

I'M COMING HOME
(Thom Bell/Linda Creed)
The Stylistics (H&L)

**IF YOU GONNA DO IT (PUT YOUR
MIND TO IT) (PART 1)**
(Leon Huff)
People's Choice (TSOP)

L.A. SUNSHINE
(Michael Burton/Phillip Terry)
War (Blue Note)

LET'S CLEAN UP THE GHETTO
(Kenny Gamble/Leon Huff/
 Cary Gilbert)
**Philadelphia International All
Stars** (Phil. Int.)

LOVING YOU–LOSING YOU
(Thom Bell/LeRoy Bell)
Phyllis Hyman (Buddah)

ME AND MY MUSIC
(Sherman Marshall/Ted Wortham)
The Spinners (Atlantic)

MY LOVE IS FREE
(Allan Felder/Bunny Sigler)
Double Exposure (Salsoul)

SEE YOU WHEN I GET THERE
(Kenny Gamble/Leon Huff)
Lou Rawls (Phil. Int.)

SHOW YOU THE WAY TO GO
(Kenny Gamble/Leon Huff)
The Jacksons (Epic)

SUNSHINE
(Bunny Sigler/Phil Hurtt)
Enchantment (Roadshow)

TAKE ME AS I AM
(Charles Simmons/Joseph Jefferson/
Bruce Hawes)
Philippe Wynne (Cotillion)

THIS SONG WILL LAST FOREVER
(Kenny Gamble/Leon Huff/
Cary Gilbert)
Lou Rawls (Phil. Int.)

WHAT WOULD THE WORLD BE WITHOUT MUSIC
(Bunny Sigler/Don Covay)
Mystique (Curtom)

WHEN LOVE IS NEW
(Kenny Gamble/Leon Huff)
Arthur Prysock (Old Town)

THE WHOLE TOWN'S LAUGHING AT ME
(Sherman Marshall/Ted Wortham)
Teddy Pendergrass (Phil. Int.)

WORK ON ME
(Kenny Gamble/Leon Huff)
The O'Jays (Phil. Int.)

YOU'LL NEVER FIND ANOTHER LOVE LIKE MINE
(Kenny Gamble/Leon Huff)
Stanley Turrentine (Fantasy)

YOU'RE THROWING A GOOD LOVE AWAY
(Sherman Marshall/Ted Wortham)
The Spinners (Atlantic)

1978

BRANDY (I REALLY MISS YOU)
(Charles Simmons/Joseph Jefferson)
The O'Jays (Phil. Int.)

CLOSE THE DOOR
(Kenny Gamble/Leon Huff)
Teddy Pendergrass (Phil. Int.)

DON'T LET IT GO TO YOUR HEAD
(Kenny Gamble/Leon Huff)
Jean Carn (TSOP)

EASY COME EASY GO
(Thom Bell/LeRoy Bell/Casey James)
The Spinners (Atlantic)

FIND ME A GIRL
(Kenny Gamble/Leon Huff)
The Jacksons (Epic)

FROM NOW ON
(Bunny Sigler)
Linda Clifford (Curtom)

I AM YOUR WOMAN SHE IS YOUR WIFE
(Barbara Mason/Weldon McDougal)
Barbara Mason (Prelude)

I'M JUST THINKING ABOUT COOLING OUT
(Kenny Gamble/Leon Huff/
Jerry Butler)
Jerry Butler (Phil. Int.)

I'VE BEEN MISSING YOU
(Douglas Brown/Tom Wallington/
John Whitehead/Gene McFadden)
Archie Bell and the Drells (Phil. Int.)

IF YOU WANNA DO A DANCE ALL NIGHT
(Thom Bell/LeRoy Bell/
Anthony Bell/Casey James)
The Spinners (Atlantic)

LADY LOVE
(Yvonne Gray/Sherman Marshall)
Lou Rawls (Phil. Int.)

ONE LIFE TO LIVE
(Kenny Gamble/Leon Huff)
Lou Rawls (Phil. Int.)

ONE NIGHT AFFAIR
(Kenny Gamble/Leon Huff)
Samona Cooke (Mercury)

ONLY THE STRONG SURVIVE
(Kenny Gamble/Leon Huff/
Jerry Butler)
Billy Paul (Phil. Int.)

ONLY YOU
(aka JESUS HE'S GOT WHAT I NEED)
(Kenny Gamble/Leon Huff)
Teddy Pendergrass (Phil. Int.)

SOLUTIONS
(Dexter Wansel/Cynthia Biggs)
Dexter Wansel (Phil. Int.)

STANDING RIGHT HERE
(John Whitehead/Gene McFadden/
Victor Carstarphen)
Melba Moore (Buddah)

THERE WILL BE LOVE
(Kenny Gamble/Leon Huff)
Lou Rawls (Phil. Int.)

USE TA BE MY GIRL
(Kenny Gamble/Leon Huff)
The O'Jays (Phil. Int.)
MFSB (Phil. Int.)

1979

AIN'T NO STOPPIN' US NOW
(Gene McFadden/John Whitehead/
Jerry Cohen)
McFadden & Whitehead (Phil. Int.)

ARE YOU READY (FOR LOVE)
(Thom Bell/LeRoy Bell/
Casey James)
The Spinners (Atlantic)

BRING THE FAMILY BACK
(Frankie Smith/Phillip Terry)
Billy Paul (Phil. Int.)

COME GO WITH ME
(Kenny Gamble/Leon Huff)
Teddy Pendergrass (Phil. Int.)

COUNT THE DAYS (aka COUNT THE DAYS GONE BY)
(Cary Gilbert/Talmadge Conway/
Allan Felder)
Al Wilson (Roadshow)

I WANNA DO THE DO
(Bobby Rush/Leon Huff)
Bobby Rush (Phil Int.)

I WANT YOU HERE WITH ME
(Kenny Gamble/Leon Huff)
The O'Jays (Phil. Int.)

IT'S BEEN COOL
(Dexter Wansel)
Dexter Wansel (Phil. Int.)

LET ME BE GOOD TO YOU
(Kenny Gamble/Leon Huff)
Lou Rawls (Phil. Int.)

LIVIN' IT UP (FRIDAY NIGHT)
(LeRoy Bell/Casey James)
Bell & James (A&M)

MAMA CAN'T BUY YOU LOVE
(LeRoy Bell/Casey James)
Elton John (MCA)

NOTHING SAYS I LOVE YOU LIKE I LOVE YOU
(Kenny Gamble/Leon Huff/
Jerry Butler)
Jerry Butler (Phil. Int.)

NOW THAT WE FOUND LOVE
(Kenny Gamble/Leon Huff)
Third World (Island)

PARTY TIME MAN
(Ted Wortham/Sherman Marshall)
The Futures (Phil. Int.)

PICK ME UP I'LL DANCE
(John Whitehead/Gene McFadden/
Ronald Rose)
Melba Moore (Epic)

SHAKEDOWN
(Casey James/LeRoy Bell)
Bell & James (A&M)

SING A HAPPY SONG
(Kenny Gamble/Leon Huff)
The O'Jays (Phil. Int.)

STRATEGY
(John Whitehead/Gene McFadden/
Jerry Cohen)
Archie Bell and the Drells
(Phil. Int.)

THERE SHE GOES AGAIN
(August Wm. Johnson/
Steve Beckmeier)
The Boppers (Fantasy)

THIS TIME BABY
(Casey James/LeRoy Bell)
Jackie Moore (Columbia)

TURN OFF THE LIGHTS
(Kenny Gamble/Leon Huff)
Teddy Pendergrass (Phil. Int.)

WE'RE A MELODY
(Dexter Wansel/Cynthia Biggs)
The Jones Girls (Phil. Int.)

WHILE WE STILL HAVE TIME
(Ted Wortham/Cynthia Biggs)
Cindy & Roy (Casablanca)

YOU ARE EVERYTING
(Thom Bell/Linda Creed)
Roberta Flack (Atlantic)

**YOU GONNA MAKE ME LOVE
SOMEBODY ELSE**
(Kenny Gamble/Leon Huff)
The Jones Girls (Phil. Int.)

YOU NEVER KNOW WHAT YOU'VE GOT
(LeRoy Bell/Casey James)
Bell & James (A&M)

1980

THE BEST LOVE I EVER HAD
(Kenny Gamble/Leon Huff)
Jerry Butler (Phil. Int.)

COWBOYS TO GIRLS
(Kenny Gamble/Leon Huff)
Philly Cream (WMOT)

DANCE TURNED INTO A ROMANCE
(Kenny Gamble/Leon Huff)
The Jones Girls (Phil. Int.)

DIDN'T I (BLOW YOUR MIND)
(Thom Bell/William Hart)
Millie Jackson (Spring)

DON'T BE AN ISLAND
(Alice Echols/Keith Echols)
Jerry Butler (Phil. Int.)

FOREVER MINE
(Kenny Gamble/Leon Huff)
The O'Jays (Phil. Int.)

GIRL DON'T LET IT GET YOU DOWN
(Kenny Gamble/Leon Huff)
The O'Jays (TSOP)

HURRY UP THIS WAY AGAIN
(Dexter Wansel/Cynthia Biggs)
The Stylistics (TSOP)

**I CAN'T STOP
(TURNING YOU ON)**
(Charles Simmons/Joseph Jefferson/
Richard Roebuck)
Silk (Phil. Int.)

I HEARD IT IN A LOVE SONG
(Gene McFadden/John Whitehead/
Jerry Cohen)
McFadden & Whitehead (TSOP)

I SHOULD BE YOUR LOVER
(Kenny Gamble/Leon Huff)
**Harold Melvin and the
Blue Notes** (Source)

I WANNA KNOW YOUR NAME
(Kenny Gamble/Leon Huff)
Frank Hooker and Positive People
(Panorama)

I'VE BEEN PUSHED ASIDE
(John Whitehead/Gene McFadden/
Jerry Cohen)
McFadden & Whitehead
(Phil. Int.)

IT'S YOU I LOVE
(Kenny Gamble/Leon Huff)
Teddy Pendergrass (Phil. Int.)

LOVE T.K.O.
(Cecil Womack/Gip Noble Jr./
Linda Womack)
Teddy Pendergrass (Phil. Int.)
David Oliver (Mercury)

LOVE WON'T LET ME WAIT
(Vinnie Barrett/Bobby Eli)
Jackie Moore (Columbia)

LOVE'S SWEET SENSATION
(F. Bleu)
**Curtis Mayfield and
Linda Clifford** (RSO)

MY LOVE DON'T COME EASY
(Eddie Lavert/Dennis Williams/
Mike Jackson)
Jean Carn (Phil. Int.)

ONCE IS NOT ENOUGH
(Bunny Sigler/Harvey Scales)
The O'Jays (TSOP)

ONE IN A MILLION (GUY)
(Thom Bell/Joseph Brickson)
Dee Dee Bridgewater (Elektra)

ONLY MAKE BELIEVE
(LeRoy Bell/Casey James)
Bell & James (A&M)

PRAYIN'
(Gene McFadden/John Whitehead)
**Harold Melvin and the
Blue Notes** (Source)

SHOUT AND SCREAM
(Kenny Gamble/Leon Huff)
Teddy Pendergrass (Phil. Int.)

SIT DOWN AND TALK TO ME
(Kenny Gamble/Leon Huff)
Lou Rawls (Phil. Int.)

THE SWEETEST PAIN
(Dexter Wansel/Cynthia Biggs)
Dexter Wansel (Phil. Int.)

TIGHT MONEY
(Leon Huff)
Leon Huff (Phil. Int.)

YOU'RE MY BLESSING
(Kenny Gamble/Leon Huff)
Lou Rawls (Phil. Int.)

YOU'RE MY SWEETNESS
(Kenny Gamble/Leon Huff)
Billy Paul (Phil. Int.)

1981

AIMING AT YOUR HEART
(Charles Simmons/Joseph Jefferson/
Richard Roebuck)
The Temptations (Gordy)

AND I'LL SEE YOU NO MORE
(Russell Thompkins/
Raymond Johnson)
The Stylistics (TSOP)

I AIN'T JIVIN' I'M JAMMIN'
(Leon Huff)
Leon Huff (Phil. Int.)

I CAN'T LIVE (WITHOUT YOUR LOVE)
(Leon Huff/Cecil Womack)
Teddy Pendergrass (Phil. Int.)

I JUST LOVE THE MAN
(Kenny Gamble/Leon Huff)
The Jones Girls (Phil. Int.)

I LOVE YOU ANYWAY
(Kenny Gamble/Dexter Wansel/
Cynthia Biggs)
Dee Dee Sharp Gamble (Phil. Int.)

IT'S YOUR CONSCIENCE
(Thom Bell/Deniece Williams)
Deniece Williams (ARC)

LA LA MEANS I LOVE YOU
(Thom Bell/William Hart)
Tierra (Boardwalk)
L.A. Boppers (Mercury)

LET'S MEND WHAT'S BEEN BROKEN
(Gene McFadden/John Whitehead/
Jerry Cohen)
Gloria Gaynor (Polydor)

LOVE DON'T LOVE NOBODY
(Joseph Jefferson/Charles Simmons)
Jean Carn (TSOP)

TOGETHER
(Kenny Gamble/Leon Huff)
Tierra (Boardwalk)

WARM WEATHER
(Dexter Wansel/Cynthia Biggs)
Pieces of a Dream (Elektra)

WHAT TWO CAN DO
(Thom Bell/Deniece Williams)
Deniece Williams (ARC)

WHAT'S YOUR NAME
(Dexter Wansel/Cynthia Biggs)
The Stylistics (TSOP)

YOU ARE EVERYTHING
(Thom Bell/Linda Creed)
Eloise Laws (Liberty)

1982

I CAN'T WIN FOR LOSING
(John Whitehead/Gene McFadden/
Victor Carstarphen)
Teddy Pendergrass (Phil. Int.)

IF YOU DON'T KNOW ME BY NOW
(Kenny Gamble/Leon Huff)
Jean Carn (Motown)

JUST BE YOURSELF
(Dexter Wansel/Cynthia Biggs)
Cameo (Choc. City)

LET'S STAND TOGETHER
(Gene McFadden/John Whitehead/
Melba Moore)
Melba Moore (EMI America)

NIGHTS OVER EGYPT
(Dexter Wansel/Cynthia Biggs)
The Jones Girls (Phil. Int.)

NINE TIMES OUT OF TEN
(Kenny Gamble/Leon Huff)
Teddy Pendergrass (Phil. Int.)

(I FOUND) THAT MAN OF MINE
(Kenny Gamble/Leon Huff)
The Jones Girls (Phil. Int.)

THIS GIFT OF LIFE
(Kenny Gamble/Leon Huff)
Teddy Pendergrass (Phil. Int.)

WAITING
(Thom Bell/Deniece Williams)
Deniece Williams (ARC)

WAITING BY THE HOTLINE
(Thom Bell/Deniece Williams)
Deniece Williams (ARC)

WILL YOU KISS ME ONE MORE TIME
(Thom Bell/Deniece Williams)
Lou Rawls (Epic)

**YOU'RE MY LATEST,
MY GREATEST INSPIRATION**
(Kenny Gamble/Leon Huff)
Teddy Pendergrass (Phil. Int.)

**YOUR BODY'S HERE WITH ME (BUT
YOUR MIND'S ON THE OTHER SIDE)**
(Bunny Sigler/James Sigler/
Cary Gilbert)
The O'Jays (Phil. Int.)

1983

THE BEST IS YET TO COME
(Dexter Wansel/Cynthia Biggs)
**Grover Washington Jr. with
Patti LaBelle** (Elektra)

DO IT ANY WAY YOU WANNA
(Leon Huff)
Cashmere (Philly W.)

I CAN'T STAND THE PAIN
(Kenny Gamble/Leon Huff)
The O'Jays (Phil. Int.)

PUT OUR HEADS TOGETHER
(Kenny Gamble/Kenneth Burke)
The O'Jays (Phil. Int.)

1984

EXTRAORDINARY GIRL
(Kenny Gamble/Leon Huff)
The O'Jays (Phil. Int.)

I WANT MY BABY BACK
(Kenny Gamble/Cecil Womack)
Teddy Pendergrass (Phil. Int.)

I'LL BE AROUND
(Thom Bell/Phil Hurtt)
Terri Wells (Philly World)

IF ONLY YOU KNEW
(Dexter Wansel/Cynthia Biggs/
Kenny Gamble)
Patti LaBelle (Phil. Int.)

**LET ME SHOW YOU
(HOW MUCH I REALLY LOVE YOU)**
(James Sigler)
The O'Jays (Phil. Int.)

LOVE, NEED AND WANT YOU
(Kenny Gamble/Bunny Sigler)
Patti LaBelle (Phil. Int.)

LOVE WON'T LET ME WAIT
(Vinnie Barrett/Bobby Eli)
**Johnny Mathis and
Deniece Williams** (Columbia)

1985

I CAN'T FORGET YOU
(Terri Wells/James Herbert Smith)
Patti LaBelle (Phil. Int.)

I'LL BE AROUND
(Thom Bell/Phil Hurtt)
What Is This (MCA)

JUST ANOTHER LONELY NIGHT
(Kenny Gamble/Leon Huff)
The O'Jays (Phil. Int.)

1986

CLOSER THAN CLOSE
(Thom Bell/Linda Creed/Preston
Glass/Alan Glass)
Jean Carne (Omni)
(previously known as Jean Carn)

COULD IT BE I'M FALLING IN LOVE
(Melvin Steals/Mervin Steals)
Jaki Graham with David Grant
(Capitol)

DO YOU GET ENOUGH LOVE
(Bunny Sigler)
Shirley Jones (Phil. Int.)

I JUMPED OUT OF MY SKIN
(Bunny Sigler/Jimmy Sigler/
Rick Finch/Marvin Mitchell)
Kenny & Johnny (Whitehead)
(Phil. Int.)

IF YOU DON'T KNOW ME BY NOW
(Kenny Gamble/Leon Huff)
Patti LaBelle (Phil. Int.)

LAST NIGHT (I NEEDED SOMEBODY)
(Kenny Gamble/Cynthia Biggs)
Shirley Jones (Phil. Int.)

NURSERY RHYMES
(Leon Huff/Cary Gilbert)
L.A. Dream Team (MCA)

OLD FRIEND
(Thom Bell/Linda Creed)
Phyllis Hyman (Phil. Int.)

STYLIN'
(John Whitehead/K. Whitehead/
Victor Carstarphen/
D. Whitehead/A. Whitehead)
Kenny & Johnny (Whitehead)
(Phil. Int.)

WHAT A WOMAN
(Bunny Sigler/Jimmy Sigler)
The O'Jays (Phil. Int.)

1987

DON'T TAKE YOUR LOVE AWAY
(Kenny Gamble/Leon Huff/
Cary Gilbert)
The O'Jays (Phil. Int.)

I WANNA KNOW YOUR NAME
(Kenny Gamble/Leon Huff)
Force M.D.'s (Tommy Boy)

LIVING ALL ALONE
(Kenny Gamble/Cynthia Biggs/
Dexter Wansel)
Phyllis Hyman (Phil. Int.)

LOVIN' YOU
(Kenny Gamble/Leon Huff)
The O'Jays (Phil. Int.)

SHE KNEW ABOUT ME
(Kenny Gamble/Shirley Jones/
Reginald Griffin)
Shirley Jones (Phil. Int.)

1988

I WISH YOU BELONGED TO ME
(Kenny Gamble/Leon Huff)
Lou Rawls (Phil. Int.)

1989

DIDN'T I (BLOW YOUR MIND THIS TIME)
(Thom Bell/William Hart)
New Kids on the Block (Columbia)

FOR THE LOVE OF MONEY
(Kenny Gamble/Leon Huff/
Arthur Jackson)
Bulletboys (Warner Bros.)

IF YOU DON'T KNOW ME BY NOW
(Kenny Gamble/Leon Huff)
Simply Red (Elektra)

1991
Partial Listing

NOW THAT WE FOUND LOVE
(Kenny Gamble/Leon Huff)
Heavy D & the Boyz (Uptown)

NATIONALLY KNOWN
POP, JAZZ, ROCK, AND R&B
RECORDING ARTISTS

FROM THE GREATER PHILADELPHIA AREA

MARIAN ANDERSON

Marian Anderson was a world-renowned contralto, with a rich and beautiful voice, who sang both opera and spirituals.

She gave her first concert at New York's Town Hall at the age of 27. After studying in London, Anderson performed extensively in Europe for 10 years. She returned to the U.S. in 1935 and became the country's third-highest concert box office draw.

In 1939, Anderson was denied a concert engagement in Washington, D.C., at Constitutional Hall, which was owned by the Daughters of the American Revolution. A national protest erupted. In support of her, First Lady Eleanor Roosevelt resigned from the DAR and urged the U.S. Department of the Interior to allow Anderson to sing at the Lincoln Memorial. Her concert drew 75,000 people and a radio audience of millions.

In 1955, at the age of 57, she made her debut with the Metropolitan Opera Company, and became a permanent member.

With a combination of dignity, serenity, talent, and perseverance, Marian Anderson passed on a rich legacy of accomplishments for artists to live up to.

LEE ANDREWS AND THE HEARTS
Lee Andrews (lead vocal), Roy Calhoun, Wendell Calhoun, Thomas "Butch" Curry, Ted Weems

As neighborhood teens in Southwest Philadelphia, Andrews,

Curry, Weems, and the Calhouns began singing in gospel groups before uniting as the Dreams. Their wonderful harmony and extraordinary talent led to an audition with WHAT D.J. Kae Williams and, in turn, Rainbow Records.

When it was proposed that a new name be given to the backup group for lead singer Andrews, a plastic heart discovered on a secretary's desk at the Reco-Arts studio (where the group recorded) became their signature.

In 1957, Lee Andrews and the Hearts recorded "Long Lonely Nights" on Mainline Records, and the song became a local hit. The record was later released on Chess Records and became a national hit. Later that year came "Teardrops" (a Top-10 R&B hit and Top-20 pop hit). In the spring of 1958, the group signed with United Artists, and that company's first release was "Try the Impossible," which was also successful nationally.

Their other memorable '50s songs include "Just Suppose," "Maybe You'll Be There," "On a Night Like Tonight," "In My Lonely Room," "Why Do I," "P.S. I Love You," and "I Wonder." In the '60s, Andrews reorganized the Hearts (now composed of Richard Booker, Robert Howard, Richard Mason, and Victoria McCalister) and continued to record throughout the decade. Local '60s hits include "I'm Sorry Pillow" (Cameo-Parkway), "Island of Love" (Crimson), "Cold Grey Dawn" (Lost Nite), "Quiet As It's Kept" (Lost Nite), and "You're Taking a Long Time Coming Back" (RCA).

For many years after, Lee Andrews and the Hearts performed to sold-out audiences at Madison Square Garden, the Spectrum, Valley Forge Music Fair, and the Claridge Casino in Atlantic City. Blessed with a smooth and melodious voice, Lee Andrews became one of the finest R&B recording artists to emerge from the '50s Philadelphia music scene.

FRANKIE AVALON

Born in South Philadelphia and tutored on the trumpet by his father, Frankie Avalon performed on local and national TV. Discovered at age 16, he launched a singing career in 1957. He had over 20 charted hits from 1958 to 1962 on Chancellor Records, among them, "Dede Dinah," "You Excite Me," "Ginger Bread," "I'll Wait for You," "Bobby Sox to Stockings," "Why," "Venus," "A Boy without a Girl," "Just Ask Your Heart," "Two Fools," "Swingin' on a Rainbow," "Don't Throw Away All Those Teardrops," "Where Are You," "Togetherness," "A Perfect Love," "All of Everything," "Who Else but You," "True True Love," "You Are Mine," "Tuxedo Junction," and "A Miracle."

Beginning a film career in the early 1960s, Avalon appeared in such films as *Guns of the Timberland*, *The Alamo*, *Voyage to the Bottom of the Sea*, *Drums of Africa*, *The Castilian*, *Beach Party*, *Muscle Beach Party*, *Bikini Beach*, *Beach Blanket Bingo*, *I'll Take Sweden*, *Fireball 500*, *Skidoo*, *The Million Eyes of Sumuru*, *The Haunted House of Horror*, *The Take*, *Grease*, *Back to the Beach*, and *Troop Beverly Hills*.

Network TV appearances include *A Dream Is a Wish Your Heart Makes—The Annette Funicello Story*; *Sabrina, the Teenage Witch*; *Full House*; *Burke's Law*; *Happy Days*; *Fantasy Island*; *The Love Boat*; *Police Story*; *Love, American Style*; *It Takes a Thief*; *The Patty Duke Show*; *The Eleventh Hour*; *Rawhide*; and others. Avalon currently tours in the musical *Grease* and appears in concert throughout the country.

Web site: www.frankieavalon.com

RICHARD BARRETT

A singer–songwriter–dancer–choreographer turned producer, Richard Barrett became one of the most successful independent black record producers and also a pioneering producer on Broadway. While working for Rama and Roulette Records in the mid- to late '50s, he discovered Frankie Lyman and the Teenagers, the Chantels, and Little Anthony and the Imperials. Upon returning to Philadelphia, he began producing the Three Degrees, who enjoyed hits well into the '70s. Barrett also worked in the late '90s, producing the group, Rap Machine.

LEN BARRY

Len Barry rose to fame as lead singer of the Dovells and, in 1963, left the group to become a solo artist. His charted hits include "1-2-3," "Like a Baby," and "Somewhere."

THOM BELL

Known for his impeccable arrangements, lush orchestration, and the resulting beautiful sound, Thom Bell helped to define the Sound of Philadelphia. From the late 1960s through the mid-1970s, he achieved great success producing and arranging for the Delfonics, Stylistics, and Spinners, resulting in twelve gold records and seven gold albums. He also contributed to the success of artists such as Harold Melvin and the Blue Notes, the O'Jays, and Jerry Butler, while working with Kenny Gamble and Leon Huff. Throughout the late '70s, '80s, and '90s, Bell worked with Johnny Mathis, Deniece Williams, Elton John, James Ingram, and Earth, Wind and Fire.

BLUE MAGIC
Vernon Sawyer, Wendell Sawyer, Keith Beaton, Theodore Mills, Richard Pratt

Blue Magic began as an R&B vocal quintet in 1972. Signed by Atlantic Records the following year, the group's first three recordings were R&B charted hits in the Top 40. In 1974, their recording of "Sideshow" went gold, became a Number-1 R&B hit, and reached a Top-10 pop list as well. Their next single, "Three Ring Circus," was also successful. Blue Magic had six more R&B charters in the mid-'70s before returning in 1981 and 1983 for several more. In 1989, they released the album, *From Out of the Blue.*

THE BLUEBELLES
Patti LaBelle, Sarah Dash, Cindy Birdsong, Nona Hendryx

The Bluebelles scored their first big hit in 1962 with "I Sold My Heart to the Junkman." Several Top-40 singles followed, among them, "Down the Aisle (Wedding Song)" and, later, "You'll Never Walk Alone" for Parkway. By late 1964, the group became known as Patti LaBelle and the Bluebelles and had two more charted songs: "All or Nothing" and "Take Me for a Little While," both on Atlantic Records.

Cindy Birdsong left the group in 1967 to join the Supremes. In the 1970s, as a trio, the group became known as LaBelle, and, in 1977, Patti LaBelle launched a solo career.

THE BLUE NOTES
Bernard Williams, Harold Melvin, Roosevelt Brodie, Jesse Gillis Jr., Franklin Peaker

Headed by Bernard Williams, the Blue Notes began in 1954. In 1956, Harold Melvin joined the group at age 16, and, in addition to performing, wrote songs, arranged, and choreographed. The group's first single, "If You Love Me" was a regional success. In 1960, they scored their first R&B charted hit with "My Hero." After Bernard Williams left and the group disassembled, Melvin put together a new version of the Blue Notes with lead singer John Atkins, Lawrence Brown, and Bernard Wilson. They returned to the charts in 1965 with "Get Out (And Let Me Cry)." The group broke up in 1969. When they got together again, Atkins did not come back, and more personnel changes followed.

(*See* Harold Melvin and the Blue Notes)

BOYZ II MEN
Nathan Morris, Wanya Morris, Shawn Stockman, Michael McCary

Boyz II Men came together in 1988, while the group's members were students at Philadelphia's High School for the Creative and Performing Arts. Their strength became soulful ballads, which showcased their smooth four-part harmonies. Some of their blockbuster hits: "End of the Road" (from the Eddie Murphy film, *Boomerang*), "Motownphilly" (from their debut album, *Cooleyhighharmony*), "It's So Hard to Say Goodbye to Yesterday" (a covered version from the film, *Cooley High*), "I'll Make Love to You" (from the hit album, *II*), "On Bended Knee" (another Number-1 hit), and "One Sweet Day" (done with Mariah Carey). Later hits: "4 Seasons of Loneliness" and "A Song for Mama" (from the 1997 album, *Evolution*) and "Pass You By" (from the album, *Nathan Michael Shawn Wanya*, in 2000).

Web site: www.boyziimen.com

BRENDA AND THE TABULATIONS
Brenda Payton, Jerry Jones, Eddie Jackson, Maurice Coates, Bernard Murphy

One of the finer soul groups of the '60s and '70s, Brenda and the Tabulations recorded some memorable ballads. "Dry Your Eyes" was their biggest hit, reaching high on both the R&B and pop charts. From 1967 to 1971, 11 of their songs reached the pop charts. The group became a trio in 1970, when Deborah Martin and Pat Mercer joined lead singer Payton. Other hits: "Right on the Tip of My Tongue" and the follow-up, "A Part of You." The group was also popular on the disco scene in the late '70s. Their release of "Let's Go All the Way (Down)" was well received on the club circuit and enjoyed some international interest as well.

SOLOMON BURKE

Solomon Burke grew up singing gospel, and, in his teens, had his own church, from which he broadcast a weekly radio show. Eventually, he signed with Atlantic Records and, a decade later, with MGM. His biggest success came in the 1960s. Among his many charted hits: "Got to Get You off My Mind," "Just Out of Reach (Of My Two Open Arms)," "Cry to Me," "Tonight's the Night," "Goodbye Baby (Baby Goodbye)," "If You Need Me," "You're Good for Me," "Proud Mary," "Take Me (Just as I Am)," "He'll Have to Go," "The Price," and "Everybody Needs Somebody to Love."

CHUBBY CHECKER

Chubby Checker was born Ernest Evans on a farm in Spring Gulley, South Carolina, but grew up in South Philadelphia. As a small boy, he saw both Sugar Child Robinson (a child piano prodigy) and famed country singer Ernest Tubb perform. Young Evans was so impressed that he vowed to enter show business someday. At age 11, he took his first step toward that goal and formed a street-corner harmony group.

By the time Evans attended South Philadelphia High School with friend Fabian Forte, he had studied piano (at the Settlement Music School) and began to do a number of vocal impressions, entertaining classmates whenever he could. After school, he sang and told jokes at the various places where he worked, such as the Produce Market (where his boss nicknamed him Chubby) and, later, at the Fresh Farm Poultry Shop on 9th Street. The owner there (Henry Colt) was so impressed with his young employee that he began to introduce him over a loudspeaker.

Colt and his friend, songwriter Kal Mann, arranged for Chubby to do a private recording for Dick Clark. (During a chance meeting with the Clarks, Clark's wife rechristened him Chubby Checker, a sly reference to Fats Domino, whom Chubby admired and imitated in his routine.) Chubby cut a yuletide novelty tune called "Jingle Bells," in which he did several impressions of top recording stars. Clark sent it to all of his friends and associates in the music business. Cameo-Parkway liked it so much that they wrote a song called "The Class," which became Chubby's first hit in early 1959.

In June of that year, Chubby recorded "The Twist." Bernie Lowe (president of Cameo-Parkway) was not initially impressed, but Checker believed "The Twist" was something special and promoted the record relentlessly. "The Twist" became a worldwide hit and introduced the concept of dancing apart to the beat.

In the early '60s, Checker became the innovator of other new dances such as "The Fly," "The Pony," and "The Hucklebuck." His recording of "Pony Time" rose to Number 1 and remained on the charts for 16 weeks.

In the fall of 1961, record history was made when Checker's original hit song, "The Twist," reentered the charts and, by January 1962, was back in the Number-1 position. (No other record has ever accomplished that feat.) His recording of "Let's Twist Again" won him a Grammy for Best Rock Performance, followed by hits such as "Slow Twistin'," "Dancin' Party," "Popeye the Hitchhiker," "The Limbo Rock," "Birdland," "Twist It Up," and "Loddy Lo." Checker's success continued for years.

Today, he continues to perform live in concert, while releasing new studio music. His maxisingle, "Limbo Rock Re-Mixes," and CD, *The Original Master of the Dance Hall Beat*, by Chubby C and OD (featuring Inner Circle) were both on *Billboard* charts, attracting a new generation.

National hits: "The Class," "The Twist," "The Hucklebuck," "Whole Lotta Shakin' Goin' On," "Pony Time," "Dance the Mess Around," "Let's Twist Again," "The Fly," "Slow Twistin'," "Dancin' Party," "Limbo Rock," "Popeye the Hitchhiker," "Let's Limbo Some More," "Twenty Miles," "Birdland," "Surf Party," "Twist It Up," "Loddy Lo," "Hooka Tooka," "Hey Bobba Needle," "Lazy Elsie Molly," "She Wants t' Swim," "Lovely Lovely," "Let's Do the Freddie," "Hey You Little Boo-Ga-Loo," and "Back in the USSR."

In recent years, apart from his musical activities, Checker

has given a "new twist" to the American snack food industry, which features several Chubby Checker snacks.

Web site: www.chubbychecker.com

CINTRON
Rocco Depersia (lead vocal), Edgardo Cintron (lead instrumental)

Cintron, a unique 15-piece band, performs an innovative blend of R&B, salsa, and Latin jazz, with full-scale harmonies, pulsating rhythms, and an inspired horn section. Their widely popular CD, *Back in the Day,* brings a refreshing feel to the contemporary music of today.

Web site: www.cintronband.com

JOHN COLTRANE

A legendary figure in jazz history, John Coltrane was known for his innovation and ardent self-expression. He learned to play alto saxophone in high school (in his native North Carolina), and, at age 16, moved with his family to Philadelphia, where he studied at the Ornstein School of Music and Granoff Studios. In the late '40s, switching to tenor saxophone, Coltrane joined Dizzie Gillespie's band and continued to play with various Philadelphia groups through the early '50s. His association with Miles Davis, who hired him in 1955, established Coltrane as an important jazz musician. During this period, he became known for playing multiple notes at one time (sheets of sound).

In 1957, Coltrane recorded for Prestige Records as a solo artist, while still performing with Davis and also recording as a sideman. By 1960, Coltrane had formed his own quartet. Hit albums: *My Favorite Things, Africa Brass, Impressions, Giant Steps,* and *A Love Supreme.*

Tragically, in 1967, Coltrane died from cancer at the age of 40. In 1982, he was posthumously awarded a Grammy for Best Jazz Performance, Soloist, for his work on the album, *Bye Bye Blackbird.* In 1997, he was given the Grammy Lifetime Achievement Award.

LINDA CREED

Linda Creed was a gifted lyricist, who paired with arranger–composer Thom Bell in the era of Philly soul. They collaborated on a number of hits for the Stylistics, such as "Stop, Look, Listen (To Your Heart)," "You Are Everything," "Betcha by Golly Wow," "I'm Stone in Love with You," and "You Make Me Feel Brand New."

Creed and Bell also created several songs for the Spinners, including the 1976 Number-1 hit, "The Rubberband Man." In 1977, Creed teamed with composer Michael Masser to write "The Greatest Love of All" for the Muhammad Ali biopic, *The Greatest.* (The song was a chart-topper for Whitney Houston in 1986.) That same year, Creed died from breast cancer in her mid-30s. She was posthumously inducted into the Songwriters Hall of Fame six years later.

JIM CROCE

Jim Croce was a gifted vocalist, guitarist, and composer. Some of his most popular songs include "Bad, Bad Leroy Brown" and "Time in a Bottle" (both reached Number 1). His other highly charted hits are "You Don't Mess Around with Jim," "I Got a Name," "Operator," and "I'll Have to Say I Love You in a Song." Croce's life and career were cut short by a fatal plane crash in 1973.

CRYSTAL MANSION

Crystal Mansion was formed by Johnny Caswell (a successful Philadelphia artist, who had a chart record with "At the Shore"). Other charted hits: "The Thought of Loving You" (written by Dave White) and "Carolina on My Mind."

DANNY AND THE JUNIORS
Danny Rapp (lead vocal), Dave White, Frank Maffei, Joe Terranova (aka Joe Terry)

A group originally called the Juvenairs got together at John Bartram High in Southwest Philadelphia. In 1957, group member Dave White wrote a song titled, "Let's All Do the Bop," a popular dance at the time. Artie Singer, of Singular Records, took the song to Dick Clark, who suggested changing the lyrics and title. The song became "At the Hop," and the group became Danny and the Juniors. "At the Hop" became a Number-1 national hit. Their follow-up song, "Rock and Roll Is Here to Stay," became an anthem for the music industry.

In the early 1960s, Dave White left the group and was replaced by Bill Carlucci. Charted hits: "At the Hop," "Sometimes (When I'm All Alone)," "Rock and Roll Is Here to Stay," "Dottie," "Twistin' USA," "Pony Express," "Back to the Hop," "Twistin' All Night Long," "Doin' the Continental Walk," and "Oo-La-La Limbo."

Today, Danny and the Juniors (led by Joe Terry) perform nationwide and recently did a European tour of England, Italy, and Austria. Their latest CD, *House on Fire*, blends pop, rock, and rockabilly. Their previous CD, *For Cool Grandkids Everywhere*, received a Top-50 Grammy Award nomination.

JAMES DARREN

Born and raised in South Philadelphia, James Darren became a familiar face to audiences all over from his work in movies, in television, and on the concert stage. After studying drama with Stella Adler in New York, he was discovered by Joyce Selznick. Darren signed a seven-year contract with Columbia Pictures and appeared in such films as *Rumble on the Docks, The Tijuana Story, The Brothers Rico, Gunmen's Walk, The Gene Krupa Story, All the Young Men, Let No Man Write My Epitaph*, and *Because They're Young*. He also played the role of Moondoggie in the film *Gidget* and returned to star in two sequels. In *Gidget*, he sang two songs, including the title tune, and became a major recording star.

Darren's next hit, "Goodbye Cruel World," reached Number 1 on the charts and received a Grammy nomination. His other Top-10 releases included "Angel Face," "Conscience," and "Her Royal Majesty."

In the early 1960s, Darren costarred with Gregory Peck, Anthony Quinn, and David Niven in *The Guns of Navarone*, and with Charlton Heston in *Diamondhead*. In 1966, he starred in the sci-fi series, *The Time Tunnel*, produced by Irwin Allen for ABC. In the 1970s, Darren toured with Buddy Hackett in concert throughout the country. He also guest-starred on TV in *Love, American Style; Police Story; Hawaii Five-O; Charlie's Angels; S.W.A.T.; The Black Sheep Squadron; Policewoman;* and *Fantasy Island*; and costarred in the television movies, *City Beneath the Sea, Lives of Jenny Dolan, Scruples, Turnover Smith,* and the feature film, *The Boss's Son.*

Darren joined the cast of the ABC series, *T. J. Hooker,* as Officer Jim Corrigan in 1982. This provided the means for his next career move—directing. From the mid-1980s on, he directed such shows as *The A-Team; Hunter; Stingray; Police Story: Gladiator School* (MOW, Movie of the Week); *Diagnosis Murder; Walker, Texas Ranger; Raven; Renegade; Nowhere Man; Beverly Hills 90210; Melrose Place;* and *Savannah*. In 1998, he was cast as Vic Fontaine on *Star Trek: Deep Space Nine*, sang four standard tunes, and became a regular. This fostered his return to singing and recording. Darren's recent CD (*Because of You*) is a tribute to many of our best-remembered pop vocalists.

Web site: www.jamesdarren.com

THE DELFONICS
William Hart (founder, lead vocal), Wilbur Hart, Randy Cain, Major Harris

Formed by William "Poogie" Hart in 1965, the Grammy Award–winning Delfonics became known for their smooth singing, rich harmony, and skillful choreography, along with a unique sound. Their most memorable songs include "La La Means I Love You," "Didn't I (Blow Your Mind This Time)," and "For the Love I Give to You," all written by William Hart. Other hits: "I'm Sorry," "Break Your Promise," "Ready or Not Here I Come (Can't Hide from Love)," "You Got Yours and I'll Get Mine," and "Trying to Make a Fool Out of Me."

Additional charted songs: "When You Get Right Down to It," "Hey! Love/Over and Over," "Somebody Loves You," "Walk Right up to the Sun," "Tell Me This Is a Dream," and "He Don't Really Love You."

Web site: www.delfonicsmusic.com

BILL DOGGETT

Bill Doggett formed his own band in 1938 and, in the late 1940s, worked as a musical arranger for Lionel Hampton, Louis Jordan, Count Basie, and Louis Armstrong. He also played piano for the Ink Spots.

In the early 1950s, Doggett formed his own combo and became known as one of the fathers of the swinging organ. In 1956, he recorded his greatest seller, the instrumental "Honky-Tonk." Other hits: "Ram-Bunk-Shush," "Soft," "Blip-Blop," "Hold It," and "Smokie."

THE DOVELLS
Len Borisoff (aka Len Barry), Jerry Gross (aka Jerry Summers), Arnie Silver (aka Arnie Satin), Mike Freda (aka Mike Dennis), Mark Gordesky (aka Mark Stevens), Jim Mealey (aka Danny Brooks)

The Dovells began singing in 1957 at local school functions. By 1961, in Bristol, just outside of Philadelphia, kids were stomping their feet to the beat of two hit songs, "Pretty Little Angel Eyes" and "Every Day of the Week," and Cameo-Parkway promoter Billy Harper brought the new dance to the attention of songwriters Dave Appell and Kal Mann. Inspired, Appell and Mann wrote "The Bristol Stomp," which became the Dovells' biggest hit. The group's other charted hits: "Do the New Continental," "Bristol Twistin' Annie," "Hully Gully Baby," "You Can't Sit Down," "Betty in Bermudas," "The Jitterbug," and "Stop Monkeyin' Around."

In 1963, Len Barry left the group to become a solo artist. (He later had the hit "1-2-3.") After his departure, the group had charted songs with "What in the World Has Come Over You," "Dancin' in the Streets," and "Here Come Da Judge" (as the Magistrates).

Today, Jerry Gross and Mark Stevens continue to perform as the Dovells, blending music and comedy to create a unique act that sets them apart from many of the standard groups from the 1960s rock 'n' roll era.

Web site: www.dovells.com

THE DREAMLOVERS
James Dunn, Clifford Dunn, Donald Hogan, Morris Gardner, Tommy Ricks, Cleveland Hammock Jr.

After backing up Chubby Checker on "The Twist," and "Let's Twist Again," the Dreamlovers became the resident backup group at Cameo-Parkway. They recorded hits with Dee Dee Sharp and the Dovells, then had a major hit of their own, "When We Get Married."

FIRST CHOICE
Rochelle Fleming (lead vocal), Joyce Jones, Annette Guest

Originally known as the Debonettes, First Choice became a Philly disco vocal group in the '70s. They achieved national acclaim with "Armed and Extremely Dangerous," which charted as both an R&B and pop hit in 1973. For the bulk of their records, First Choice was backed by the rhythm section of guitarist Norman Harris (who also produced them), bassist Ron Baker, and drummer Earl Young (the core members of MFSB, the house band at Philadelphia International Records). Their next single, "The Player, Part I," reached Number 7 on the R&B charts. Other hits: "Gotta Get Away

(From You Baby)," "Let Him Go," and "Doctor Love." Rochelle Fleming was said to have been one of the most distinctive lead vocalists in the '70s.

EDDIE FISHER

As a child, Eddie Fisher sang in amateur singing contests and, later, as a teen, in local South Philadelphia clubs. In 1949, Fisher was discovered by Eddie Cantor while singing at Grossinger's Resort Hotel in the Catskills. In 1950, he signed a recording contract with RCA Victor and had his first hit: "Thinking of You." In the early 1950s, Fisher became one of the most popular recording artists in the country.

His many hits include "Bring Back the Thrill," "Unless," "I'll Hold You in My Heart," "Turn Back the Hand of Time," "Anytime," "Tell Me Why," "Forgive Me," "I'm Yours," "Wish You Were Here," "Lady of Spain," "Even Now," Downhearted," "I'm Walking Behind You," "With These Hands," "Many Times," "Oh My Papa," "A Girl, a Girl," "I Need You Now," "Count Your Blessings," "Heart," "Song of the Dreamer/Don't Stay Away Too Long," "Dungaree Doll," "On the Street Where You Live," " Cindy, Oh Cindy," and "Tonight."

FABIAN FORTE

Discovered in his teens in 1958, Fabian was still a student at South Philadelphia High. His first release that year was a local hit called "Lillie Lou." In 1959, he had a major hit with "I'm a Man" and followed that with another huge hit, "Turn Me Loose." Possessing a magnetic presence, he became a teenage idol and had a successful recording career with 10 charted hits in a two-year period.

In the early 1960s, Fabian turned his attention toward acting. He costarred in 30 feature films and guest-starred on many network television series. In recent years, he has produced his own concert series for pay-per-view, public TV, and syndication, and continues to make personal appearances throughout the country.

Charted hits: "I'm a Man," "Turn Me Loose," "Tiger," "Come On and Get Me," "Got the Feeling," "Hound Dog Man," "This Friendly World," "String Along," "About This Thing Called Love," and "Kissin' and Twistin'."

Film credits: *North to Alaska, High Time, Mr. Hobbs Takes a Vacation, Dear Brigette, The Longest Day, Agatha Christie's Ten Little Indians, Hound Dog Man, Thunder Alley, The Second Time Around, Wild Racers, Little Laura and Big John, Jules Verne's Five Weeks in a Balloon*, and *A Bullet for Pretty Boy*.

Television appearances: *Bus Stop; Wagon Train; The Virginian; The Eleventh Hour; The Rat Patrol; The FBI; Love, American Style; Laverne and Shirley; Facts of Life; Fantasy Island; The Love Boat; Murphy Brown; Blossom; Crisis in Mid-Air* (MOW, Movie of the Week); *Disco Fever* (MOW); *Katie: Portrait of a Centerfold* (MOW); *Getting Married* (MOW); *Runaway Daughters* (MOW); and *Mr. Rock 'n' Roll: The Alan Freed Story* (MOW).

Web site:fabianforte.com

FOUR ACES
Al Alberts (lead vocal), Dave Mahoney, Sol Vaccaro, Lou Silvestri

After recording "Sin" in 1951, the Four Aces were signed by Decca Records and, with their next hit, "Tell Me Why," became very popular nationwide. Their songs were featured as title tunes in four motion pictures. In 1955, their recording of the title tune from the film, *Love Is a Many-Splendored Thing*, became a Number-1 hit.

Al Alberts left the group in the mid-1950s to become a solo act.

In addition to the above-mentioned songs, other hits by the Four Aces: "A Garden in the Rain," "Perfidia," "I'm Yours," "Should I," "Heart and Soul," "Stranger in Paradise," "The Gang That Sang Heart of My Heart," "Three Coins in the Fountain," "Wedding Bells (Are Breaking Up That Old Gang of Mine)," "It's a Woman's World," "Mister Sandman," "Melody of Love," "Heart," "A Woman in Love," "If You Can Dream," "To Love Again," "I Only Know I Love You," "Friendly Persuasion," "Someone to Love," "Written on the Wind," "Rock and Roll Rhapsody," "The World Outside," and "No Other Arms, No Other Lips."

SUNNY GALE

Raised in a South Philadelphia neighborhood of future singers, Sunny Gale became a successful recording artist in the prerock 1950s. Although other artists covered a number of her songs, she became a solid hit-maker for RCA Victor. Her releases include "Let Me Go Lover!" "C'est la Vie," "Rock and Roll Wedding," "I Laughed at Love," "Teardrops on My Pillow," "A Stolen Waltz," "Love Me Again," "Before It's Too Late," and "Goodnight Sweetheart Goodnight." Gale continued recording until the early 1960s.

KENNY GAMBLE AND LEON HUFF

Kenny Gamble and Leon Huff were the major creators (along with Thom Bell) of the Sound of Philadelphia, which became one of the most influential musical developments of the 1970s. Their initial coproduction was "The 81," a 1964 single by Candy and the Kisses. After regional success with the Intruders, they scored a Top-5 pop hit with the Soul Survivors' "Expressway to Your Heart." Achieving further recognition with Archie Bell and the Drells and Jerry Butler on Atlantic and Mercury Records, Gamble and Huff opened Philadelphia International Records in 1971.

Throughout the 1970s, they produced hit after major hit, such as Billy Paul's "Me and Mrs. Jones," Harold Melvin and the Blue Notes' "If You Don't Know Me by Now," and the O'Jays' "Backstabbers" and "Love Train." Their music provided the design for the rise of disco during the mid- to late '70s. As the premier producers of Philly soul, they have, separately and together, written and produced over 170 gold and platinum records.

Web site: gamble-huffmusic.com

STAN GETZ

Stan Getz was a renowned tenor saxophonist, who became known as "The Sound." As a teenager during the war years, he played with a variety of swing bands, doing stints with Stan Kenton, Jimmy Dorsey, and Benny Goodman. Getz earned acclaim during his time with Woody Herman's Second Herd in the late '40s, soloing on "Four Brothers" and being prominently featured on "Early Autumn." After his years with Herman, he became a leader for the remainder of his music career.

Already extremely popular by the early '50s, Getz brought attention to the bossa nova in the early '60s with his recording of *Jazz Samba* (with Charlie Byrd) and "The Girl from Ipanema" (a collaboration with João Gilberto and Antonio Carlos Jobim). In the mid- to late '60's, he played throughout the soundtrack of the feature film, *Mickey One* (directed by Philadelphia's Arthur Penn, starring Warren Beatty), and recorded the album, *Sweet Rain* (with Chick Corea). His '70s work includes *Dynasty* (with Eddy Louiss), *Captain Marvel* (with Chick Corea), and *The Peacocks* (with Jimmy Rowles). Getz's final recording was 1991's *People Time* (with pianist Kenny Baron).

CHARLIE GRACIE

Charlie Gracie first learned to play guitar as a youth growing up in South Philadelphia. At age 14, he made an impressive debut on Paul Whiteman's *TV Teen Club* and became a regular on the show for two years. Gracie recorded, in 1951, what some consider the first rock 'n' roll record: "Boogie Woogie Blues." In 1957, at 20 years old, he cut "Butterfly," written by Bernie Lowe and Kal Mann, which became a Number-1 hit and sold over 3 million copies in the U.S. and U.K. The flip side, "99 Ways," charted at Number 11 to make the record a double-sided hit. His follow-up, "Fabulous," reached Number 16 on the charts, to give him three top-rated releases in the same year.

Gracie also achieved great success in England, where his recordings of "I Love You So Much It Hurts," "Wanderin' Eyes," and "Cool Baby" were huge hits.

Known as a virtuoso guitar player, he was highly admired by George Harrison, Van Morrison, and Paul McCartney, who recorded "Fabulous" on one of his recent albums. Gracie still performs for large audiences throughout Europe and England. His most recent CDs include *I'm All Right* (on Lanark Records) and *Just Hangin' Around* (recorded in Berlin in 2004).

Web site: www.charliegracie.com

VIVIAN GREEN

Vivian Green, who grew up in the City of Brotherly Love, began playing piano, singing, and writing songs at an early age. At 13, she joined a female group called Younique.

Eventually, her work as a backup singer for Jill Scott attracted notice and led to a contract with Columbia in late 2001. Green's first album, *A Love Story*, debuted in 2002, and her next, *Vivian*, was released in 2005.

Web site: www.viviangreen.com

BUDDY GRECO

As a singer, songwriter, arranger, and producer, Buddy Greco has enjoyed a lengthy and prolific career, cutting 70 albums and over 100 singles. Born in South Philadelphia, he studied piano at the Philadelphia Settlement House, and, at age 15, had his own musical group. In 1946, his trio (Buddy Greco with the Sharps) had their first big hit, "Oh Look at Her, Ain't She Pretty." Other hits: "The Lady Is a Tramp" and "Around the World." He joined the Benny Goodman Band, in 1948, as a piano player, vocalist, and arranger.

In the early 1950s, Greco appeared on TV and wrote songs for artists Rosemary Clooney and Eileen Barton. He cut a dozen songs for Coral Records between 1951 and 1955, including the best-seller, "I Ran All the Way Home." In the 1960s, he recorded a number of popular albums and, in 1967, had his own TV series on CBS with Buddy Rich, called *Away We Go.*

In the 1970s, Greco moved to Europe and performed around the world. After returning to the U.S., he continued to perform, produce, write, and arrange. A class entertainer, he toured in the '90s with the Salute to Benny Goodman Band.

BILL HALEY AND HIS COMETS
Bill Haley, Billy Williamson (steel guitar), Franny Beecher (lead guitar), Johnny Grande (accordion, piano), Marshall Lytle (Bass), Joey Ambrose (sax), Dick Richards (drums)

Bill Haley and His Comets had their first hit, in 1953, with "Crazy Man Crazy." The following year, they had two million-sellers in "Shake Rattle and Roll" and "Dim Dim the Lights." In 1955, a song they had recorded over a year earlier, "(We're Gonna) Rock around the Clock," found new life as the theme song for the movie, *Blackboard Jungle*, and became Number 1 in the world. Often called the father of rock 'n' roll, Haley paved the way for many other artists.

Charted hits: "Crazy Man Crazy," "Shake Rattle and Roll," "Dim Dim the Lights," "Mambo Rock," "Birth of the Boogie," "(We're Gonna) Rock around the Clock," "Razzle Dazzle," "Two Hound Dogs," "Burn That Candle," "See You Later Alligator," "Rock," "The Saints Rock 'n' Roll," "Hot Dog Buddy Buddy," "Rip It Up," "Rudy's Rock," "Forty Cups of Coffee," "Billy Goat," "Skinny Minnie," "Lean Jean," and "Joey's Song."

HALL AND OATES
Daryl Hall, John Oates

In the late '60s, Daryl Hall and John Oates first met at Adelphia Ballroom's big soul revue record hop in Philadelphia. Both were on the bill with different groups. Hall and Oates began recording together in 1972, with their first charted single, "She's Gone," in 1974, followed by "Sara Smile," in 1976. The next year, their recording of "Rich Girl" rose to Number 1, after which came six more charted hits.

In the 1980s, Hall and Oates became the top rock duo of the decade with five Number-1 songs: "Kiss On My List," "I Can't Go For That," "Private Eyes," "Maneater," and "Out of Touch." Their Top-10 hits include "You Make My Dreams," "Do It in a Minute," "One on One," "Family Man," "Say It Isn't So," "Adult Education," "Method of Modern Love," and "Everything Your Heart Desires."

In recent years, they recorded the albums, *Do It for Love* (2002) and *Our Kind of Soul* (2004), the latter featuring a number of Philly soul classics with new arrangements.

EDDIE HOLMAN

While attending Overbrook High School in the early 1960s, Eddie Holman began to write, produce, and record. His first charted hit was "This Can't Be True Girl," and other popular recordings include "Eternal Love," "Time Will Tell," "It's All in the Game," "I Love You," "United," and "Don't Stop Now." His recording of "Hey There Lonely Girl" is one of the top-selling and best-remembered romantic ballads of all time. Holman's falsetto style of singing has earned him a unique place in soul music history. Today, he travels internationally with the Eddie Holman Band.

Web site: www.eddieholman.com

THE HOOTERS
Ron Hyman (vocal/guitar), Eric Brazilian (vocal/keyboard), John Lilley (guitar), Ron Miller (bass), David Uosikkinen (drums)

The Hooters, blending rock and folk, were a very popular group in the 1980s. Their hit albums include *Nervous Night*, and *One Way Home*. Hyman and Brazilian remain prolific songwriters and arrangers for some of our top recording artists.

THE INTRUDERS
Sam "Little Sonny" Brown, Eugene "Bird" Daughtry, Phillip "Phil" Terry, Robert "Big Sonny" Edwards

The four Philadelphians who became the Intruders began singing together in the early 1960s. The group's blend of Philly street-corner doo-wop tradition with Black gospel influence attracted Kenny Gamble and Leon Huff, who signed them to Gamble Records. In 1970, Robert "Bobby Star" Ferguson joined the group. Some of their biggest hits: "Cowboys to Girls," "(Love Is like a) Baseball Game," "When We Get Married," and "I'll Always Love My Mama (Part I)." Other charted songs: "Sad Girl," "Together," "Slow Drag," "I Wanna Know Your Name," "Baby I'm Lonely/A Love That's Real," and "(We'll Be) United."

JAY AND THE TECHNIQUES
Jay Proctor, Karl Landis, Ronnie Goosly, John Walsh, George Lloyd, Chuck Crowl, Dante Dancho

In 1967, Jay and the Techniques recorded the catchy, upbeat "Apples, Peaches, Pumpkin Pie," which became a Top-10 R&B

and pop hit, remaining on the charts for 11 weeks (the song is still very popular among collectors). A subsequent song, "Baby Make Your Own Sweet Music," had success in the U.K.

JOAN JETT

Originally from Philadelphia, Joan Jett became an icon for scores of female rockers. At age 15, she created her first band (eventually called the Runaways) and recorded three albums for Mercury Records. Jett moved to New York to launch a solo career in the 1980s and, during this period, also formed the Blackhearts. Her greatest hits include "I Love Rock 'n' Roll," "Crimson and Clover" (a covered version), and "I Hate Myself for Loving You." In the mid-'90s, she scored with the album, *Pure and Simple*, and, in 1999, reunited with the Blackhearts, recording the album, *Fetish*.

Web site: www.joanjett.com

JODIMARS
Joey Ambrose, Dick Richards, Marshall Lytle

After leaving Bill Haley & His Comets in late 1955, Joey Ambrose, Dick Richards, and Marshall Lytle formed their own group, calling themselves Jodimars, an acronym of their first names. They signed with Capitol Records in 1956, and their first release, "Now Dig This," was a national hit. "Let's All Rock Together" and "Clarabella" (which was later recorded by the Beatles and used in their concert series) followed.

In the late '50s, Jodimars became one of the top lounge acts in Las Vegas and Reno. They also enjoyed widespread popularity in Europe and the U.K., where *Now Dig This* became the title of the well-known English rock magazine.

LOUIS JORDAN

An entertaining alto saxophonist, Louis Jordan was one of the originators of the jump blues in the 1940s, which became the blueprint for rock 'n' roll. Between 1942 and 1951, Jordan, who was among the first black entertainers to sell in the pop sector, had 57 R&B chart hits on Decca Records. Some of his classic works: "Buzz Me," "Caldonia," "G.I. Jive," "Choo Choo Ch'Boogie," "Ain't That Just like a Woman," "Ain't Nobody Here but Us Chickens," "Boogie Woogie Blue Plate," "Beans and Cornbread," "Saturday Night Fish Fry," and "Blue Light Boogie."

KITTY KALLEN

As a youth, Kitty Kallen performed on the *Children's Hour* on WCAU radio and was discovered by bandleader Gil Fitch, who also played for the SPHAS (Philadelphia's first pro basketball team). In the late 1930s, she was a teenage songstress with Fitch and his band at the Broadwood Hotel after Saturday-night SPHA games.

Kallen became a band singer, in the 1940s, with Jimmy Dorsey and Harry James. In the early 1950s, she signed with Decca Records and, in 1954, had a Number-1 hit with "Little Things Mean a Lot." After a brief retirement, in the late '50s, she signed with Columbia Records and had a hit soon after, called "If I Give My Heart to You." Other charted songs: "In the Chapel in the Moonlight," "I Want You All to Myself," "Go on with the Wedding" (with Georgie Shaw), and "My Coloring Book."

KEITH

Keith (born James Barry Keefer) first rose to prominence in 1966 with the release of "Ain't Gonna Lie" (on Mercury Records), which made the Top 40. In 1967, his recording of "98.6" cracked the Top 10; his last national hit was "Tell Me to My Face." After recording his final album *The Adventures of Keith* (for RCA) in 1969, he staged a brief comeback in the mid-'80s.

EVELYN "CHAMPAGNE" KING

Evelyn King began singing in her teens and, ironically, was discovered while working as a cleaning lady at Philadelphia International—she was filling in for her sister—by producer T. Life. A contract with RCA followed. Her recording of the million-seller, "Shame," reaching the Top 10 on both the R&B and pop charts in 1978, put her in the spotlight. King's follow-up, "I Don't Know If It's Right," placed high on the charts and also went gold. "I'm in Love" and "Love Comes Down" both scored as Number-1 R&B hits in the early '80s; "Hold On" was a Top-10 hit. Her hit LPs include *Smooth Talk, Call on Me, I'm in Love,* and *Get Loose.*

Web site: www.evelynchampagneking.com

PATTI LABELLE

Born and raised in the melting pot of Southwest Philadelphia, Patti LaBelle has enjoyed a long-lasting musical career. She grew up singing in a local Baptist choir and, in the early 1960s, became the lead singer of the Bluebelles, which had four charted hits by 1965. LaBelle launched a solo career in the 1970s and has amassed over 30 charted singles, including 1975's "Lady Marmalade"; 1983's chart topper, "If Only You Knew"; the 1985 hit, "New Attitude"; a pop and R&B Number-1 single, "On My Own" (which was a 1986 duet with Michael McDonald); and more recent hits like "Somebody Loves You Baby," "When You've Been Blessed," "The Right Kind of Lover," and "When You Talk About Love."

Among LaBelle's solo works are the platinum-selling "Winner in You" and three gold albums, *Burnin', Gems,* and *Flame.* LaBelle has also authored four books, one of which is her best-selling autobiography, *Don't Block the Blessings.* A multiple Grammy Award winner, she last received a nomination in 2003 for the inspirational hit, "Way Up There." She recently recorded the album, *Timeless Journey*, and began hosting a new TV series, *Living It Up.*

Web site: www.pattilabelle.com

MARIO LANZA

A native of South Philadelphia, Mario Lanza began singing as a teenager in his high school choir. After serving in the military, he returned home and signed a 10-year recording contract with RCA Victor. In 1949, he made his film debut for MGM in *That Midnight Kiss*. The following year, in the film, *The Toast of New Orleans*, Lanza sang "Be My Love," which became a Number-1 national hit in 1951. A year later, his portrayal of Enrico Caruso in *The Great Caruso* brought him worldwide recognition.

Lanza went to Europe in the late 1950s to make a series of films. In 1959, he died of a heart attack at age 38. His greatest hits include "Be My Love," "Celeste Aida," "The Loveliest Night of the Year," "Because You're Mine," "Earthbound," and "Arrivederci Roma."

GLORIA MANN

Gloria Mann was one of the better-known female vocalists to emerge from Philadelphia in the mid-1950s. Her recordings of "Earth Angel" and "Teenage Prayer" placed in the Top 20, but because other artists covered some of her best work, Mann never reached the megastardom she might have achieved.

PEGGY MARCH

Peggy March, who began singing as a child and was a regular on the Rex Trailer TV show in the mid-1950s, sang in local bands. In 1963, while still a high school student, she recorded "I Will Follow Him" for RCA, which became a Number-1 hit. Other charted hits: "I Wish I Were a Princess," "Hello Heartache Goodbye Love," "The Impossible Happened," and "(I'm Watching) Every Little Move You Make."

The success of "I Will Follow Him" gave March opportunities abroad, and she began to record in Dutch, Italian, Spanish, Japanese, and German. Through the 1960s, she continually topped the German charts and enjoyed success in Japan as well.

March lived in Germany in the 1970s and began writing songs. In 1981, she coauthored two hits: "Manuel Goodbye" and "When the Rain Begins to Fall." She eventually returned to the U.S. and continues to appear in concert. In recent years, March has become an accomplished painter.

AL MARTINO

One of South Philadelphia's finest pop singers, Al Martino began his recording career with Capitol Records in 1952. His first hit, "Here in My Heart," went to Number 1. Other charted hits in the 1950s and 1960s: "I Can't Get You Out of My Heart," "Darling I Love You," "I Love You Because," "Painted Tainted Rose," "Living a Lie," "I Love You More and More Every Day," "Always Together," "Tears And Roses," and "We Could." In 1966, he recorded "Spanish Eyes," which became his signature song.

Martino's portrayal of Johnny Fontaine in *The Godfather* and his recording of "Speak Softly Love" (the film's love theme) refreshed his career in the 1970s. He continued to perform in clubs, lounges, and casinos throughout the country in the 1980s and 1990s. In 2000, he recorded the album *Style* and, in 2004, *Come Share the Wine*.

Web site: www.almartino.com

BARBARA MASON

Beginning as a teenage songwriter, Barbara Mason was referred to by some as Philadelphia's First Lady of Soul. In 1965, she wrote and recorded "Yes I'm Ready," which placed her in the national spotlight. Other charted hits: the follow-up, "Sad, Sad Girl," "Give Me Your Love," and "From His Woman to You." Additional songs that hit the pop charts: "If You Don't (Love Me, Tell Me So)," "Is It Me," "I Need Love," "Oh How It Hurts," "Bed and Bored," and "Shackin' Up."

Web site: www.barbaramasonmusic.com

JEANETTE MCDONALD

A native of West Philadelphia, Jeanette McDonald sang opera, operetta, and show tunes, with the ideal of popularizing classical music. At the height of her career, she became the leading female music star at MGM, entertaining audiences with her performances of classical themes, and moving them with her acting ability in romantic storylines. In her later years, McDonald combined concert work with television appearances and nightclub performances.

MCFADDEN AND WHITEHEAD
Gene McFadden, John Whitehead

Prominent songwriters and producers at Philadelphia International during the '70s, Gene McFadden and John Whitehead had a Number-1 R&B hit as vocalists: "Ain't No Stoppin' Us Now," in 1979. They also composed and produced the hits, "Backstabbers" (O'Jays) and "Bad Luck" and "Wake Up Everybody" (Harold Melvin and the Blue Notes); and produced the album, *McFadden and Whitehead*, in 1979, followed by more singles for TSOP in 1980. That same year, "I Heard It in a Love Song" was an R&B hit.

HAROLD MELVIN AND THE BLUE NOTES
Teddy Pendergrass (lead vocal), Harold Melvin, Lawrence Brown, Bernard Wilson, Lloyd Parks, Sharon Paige

During their glory years at Philadelphia International in the early to mid-'70s, Harold Melvin and the Blue Notes' main attraction was lead singer Teddy Pendergrass. Among the group's hits: "I Miss You (Part I)," "If You Don't' Know Me by Now," "The Love I Lost," "Bad Luck (Part I)," and "Wake Up Everybody." Other charted songs: "Satisfaction Guaranteed," "Where Are All My Friends," "Tell the World How I Feel About'cha Baby," and "Reaching for the World."

The group is known today as Harold Melvin's Original Blue Notes.

Telephone: 215.978.5497

MFSB (MOTHER FATHER SISTER BROTHER)
Norman Harris (guitar), Ronnie Baker (bass), Earl Young (drums), Larry Washington (percussion), Zach Zachery (sax), Vince Montana (vibes), Leonard Pakula (keyboard), Don Renaldo (strings and horns); also, Roland Chambers (guitar), Karl Chambers (drums), Bobby Eli (guitar), Richie Rome (piano); later, T. J. Tindall (guitar), Dexter Wansel (keyboard), Ron Kersey (keyboard), Charles Collins (drums), and Victor Carstarphen (piano)

MFSB became known as the house band for Philadelphia International Records. Richie Rome, Dexter Wansel, and Victor Carstarphen also did arrangements, in addition to mainstays Thom Bell, Bobby Martin, and Jack Faith.

GARNET MIMMS
Coming to Philadelphia at an early age, Garnet Mimms began singing in church as a boy and later performed with several gospel groups in his teen years. In the early 1960s, he put together Garnet Mimms and the Enchanters, recording "Cry Baby," which became a Top-5 pop hit and Number-1 R&B hit in 1963. His follow-up, a covered version of Jerry Butler's "For Your Precious Love," and the flip side, "Baby Don't You Weep," both reached the pop Top 40. His later charted hits as a solo artist include "It Was Easier to Hurt Her" and "I'll Take Good Care of You." Mimms is considered to be one of the pioneer soul singers.

THE ORLONS
Shirley Brickley, Rosetta Hightower, Marlena Davis, Stephen Caldwell

While in their teens at Overbrook High, Shirley Brickley, Rosetta Hightower, Marlena Davis, and Stephen Caldwell began to appear in talent shows at school with a group called the Cashmeres (who became the Dovells). While they were looking for a name of their own, Steve Caldwell showed his group a black orlon sweater, which inspired them to call themselves the Orlons (echoing the Cashmeres).

Len Barry, lead singer of the Dovells, arranged an audition for the group with Cameo. At the first audition, Caldwell sang lead, with the three girls backgrounding. Cameo-Parkway requested a second audition, during which Brickley, Hightower, and Davis each led a song. The group was then signed to a contract.

The Orlons' first release, "I'll Be True," was a local hit, with Davis singing lead. Their second local hit, "Mr. Twenty One," had Brickley in the lead. Their biggest seller came in 1962, with Hightower singing lead on "Wah Watusi," written by Dave Appell and Kal Mann.

Other charted hits: "Don't Hang Up," "South Street," "Not Me," "Crossfire," "Bon-Doo-Wah," "Shimmy Shimmy," "Rules of Love," and "Knock-Knock."

E-mail address: goodmusic.1@netzero.com

BILLY PAUL

Billy Paul began performing on radio broadcasts at age 11, and, at age 16, was discovered by Charlie Parker. Working with Parker, Dinah Washington, Miles Davis, John Coltrane, Roberta Flack, and Nina Simone, he grew up with an extensive jazz background. Paul's original 1959 recording of "Ebony Woman" was later re-recorded for Neptune as the title of his 1970 LP. He signed with Philadelphia International in 1971 and scored his biggest hit the following year, with "Me and Mrs. Jones" (a Grammy winner that topped both the R&B and pop charts). Two years later, Paul had another Top-10 R&B single: "Thanks for Saving My Life." He remained with Philadelphia International until the mid-'80s. He has continued to record to this day, and his latest album debuted in 2006.

Some of his many acclaimed albums: *Feelin' Good at the Cadillac Club* (re-released by Philadelphia International in 1973), *Ebony Woman, Going East, 360 Degrees of Billy Paul, War of the Gods, Billy Paul Live in Europe, Got My Head on Straight, Let 'em In, Only the Strong Survive,* and *When Love Is New.*

Web site: www.billypaul.com

MIKE PEDICIN

A talented saxophonist, Mike Pedicin made numerous appearances on *American Bandstand* and had two charted hits in the mid-1950s: "Large, Large House" (RCA) and "Shake a Hand" (Cameo).

TEDDY PENDERGRASS

In the early 1970s, Teddy Pendergrass became the lead singer of Harold Melvin and the Blue Notes. He left the group in 1976 to go solo and, with a surging baritone, became one of the top R&B artists in the country. His first three albums went gold or platinum. A 1982 car accident left him partially paralyzed, but after a year of rehabilitation, he returned to the music scene. Pendergrass continued to record albums through the 1980s and 1990s, some of which went gold. Among his many charted songs: "I Don't Love You Anymore," "You Can't Hide from Yourself," "The More I Get the More I Want," "Close the Door," "Come Go with Me," "It's You I Love," "Turn Off the Lights," "Can't We Try," "Love T.K.O.," "Shout and Scream," "I Can't Live (Without Your Love)," "This Gift of Life," and "You're My Latest, My Greatest Inspiration."

Web site: www.teddypendergrass.com

PURPLE REIGN
Paul Beato, Richie Benatti, Dave Ruczynski, Danny Reilly, Bob Beato, Kenny Cubicciotti

Beginning as a nightclub act in 1969, Paul Beato, Richie Benatti, Dave Ruczynski, Danny Reilly, Bob Beato, and Kenny Cubicciotti performed R&B songs all over the Delaware Valley. When an Atlantic Records promoter persuaded the band to do a disco version of "This Old Man," the group attained national prominence. Other charted hits:

"Love Shortage" and "You Gave Me Somebody to Love."

Telephone: BB Productions, 215.322.1960

DIANE RENAY

Diane Renay began recording as a teenager under the guidance of producer–songwriter Bob Crewe. Her debut single, "Navy Blue," was issued in 1964 and rose to Number 6 on the pop charts later that year. Her follow-up, "Kiss Me Sailor," made the Top 30. Some quality efforts followed, such as "Grown Up Too Fast" and "It's in Your Tears." Renay's LP, *Navy Blue*, rode the charts for three months. She later recorded for MGM Records, then ATCO and New Voice.

Web site: www.dianerenay.com

THE ROOTS

Ahmir Khalib Thompson (aka ?uestlove, drums), Tariq Trotter (aka Black Thought, vocal), Leon Hubbard (aka Hub, bass guitar), Kamal (keyboard), Knuckles (percussion), Kirk Douglas (aka Captain Kirk, guitar)

First getting together in 1987 in Philadelphia, the group called the Roots became synonymous with unique lyrics and live concert instrumentals, traits that inspired later hip-hop and R&B performers. Their first album, *Organix*, was released in 1993, and their 1996 release, *Illadelph Halflife*, was a Top-40 hit on *Billboard's* album chart. In 1999, the Roots accepted a Grammy for "You Got Me," a duet with R&B singer Erykah Badu (from their album, *Things Fall Apart*).

Phrenology, released in 2002, brought them a Grammy nomination, this time for Best Rap Album. Two more Grammy nominations followed, in 2004, for "Star" and "Don't Say Nuthin'," tracks from *The Tipping Point*. In 2006, the Roots released *The Game Theory* on Def Jam Records.

TODD RUNDGREN

Formerly the lead of the groups Nazz and Utopia, Todd Rundgren became a virtuoso musician, songwriter, and producer. His megahits include "Hello It's Me," "I Saw the Light," and "We Gotta Get You a Woman." Other charted songs: "Couldn't I Just Tell You," "A Dream Goes On Forever," "Real Man," "Be Nice to Me," "Good Vibrations," and "Can We Still Be Friends."

BOBBY RYDELL

Bobby Rydell learned to play drums as a child after seeing Gene Krupa at the Earle Theater, and, by age 10, was a regular on Paul Whiteman's *TV Teen Club* on WFIL. As a teen, he played drums, sang, and did impersonations in a group called Rocco and the Saints. Rydell signed with Cameo Records in 1959 at age 17, scored big with the record, "Kissin' Time," and had over 20 charted hits, including million-sellers, such as "Wild One," "Volare," and "Forget Him."

In 1963, Rydell costarred with Ann-Margret in the film version of *Bye Bye Birdie*. On television, he appeared on the *Red Skelton Show* and in dramatic series, such as *Combat*. He later recorded with Capitol Records and, in the 1970s, moved more into pop. In the 1980s, Rydell joined Frankie Avalon and Fabian on a national tour. He appeared in big-band–style concert dates and on a number of TV specials in the 1990s.

Charted hits: "Kissin' Time," "We Got Love," "I Dig Girls," "Wild One," "Little Bitty Girl," "Swingin' School," "Ding-a-Ling," "Volare," "Sway," "Goodtime Baby," "I've Got Bonnie," "I'll Never Dance Again," "That Old Black Magic," "I Wanna Thank You," "The Fish," "The Cha-Cha-Cha," "Butterfly Baby," "Wildwood Days," "Forget Him," "Make Me Forget," "A World without Love," "I Just Can't Say Goodbye," and "Diana."

Web site: www.bobbyrydell.com

JODIE SANDS

Bob Marcucci and Peter DeAngelis discovered Jodie Sands in 1957. Her recording of "With All My Heart" became one of the first hits for Chancellor Records, and the follow-up, "Someday," was also a national hit.

JILL SCOTT

North Philadelphia native Jill Scott first began performing by reading her own poetry. One listener was Roots drummer, Ahmir Thompson, who invited her to a group session and, later, collaborated with her on "You Got Me," a Top-40 hit in 1999. After a Canadian tour with the musical, *Rent*, Scott

signed a contract with the Hidden Beach label. Her first album, *Who Is Jill Scott? Words and Sounds, Vol. 1*, came out in July 2000, and her second album, *Experience: Jill Scott 826+*, a year later. In 2003, Scott earned a Grammy nomination for Best Female Vocal Performance for her single, "A Long Walk." Her third album, *Beautifully Human: Words and Sounds, Vol. 2*, was released in 2004.

Web site: www.jillscott.com

THE SENSATIONS
Yvonne Baker (lead vocal), Richard Curtain, Sam Armstrong, Alphonso Howell

In the mid-1950s, Yvonne Baker and Alphonso Howell formed the Sensations and had a hit with "Yes Sir, That's My Baby," for Atco Records. Baker retired but rejoined the group in 1961. That summer they recorded "Music, Music, Music," for Argo Records, and made the national charts. Their biggest hit came the following year with a song written by Yvonne Baker, called "Let Me In." They recorded their final hit that year with "That's My Desire."

DEE DEE SHARP

Dee Dee Sharp, who grew up in North Philadelphia and learned to play the piano by age 10, began directing the choir at the church of her grandfather, Pastor Eubie Gilbert. At age 12, when her mother was severely injured in an automobile accident, Sharp looked for work to help her family. She answered a newspaper ad and became a background singer to Willa Ward (sister of Clara Ward, the first gospel singer to appear in nightclubs). With the skills she developed, Sharp worked on sessions with Frankie Avalon, Fabian, Bobby Rydell, and Chubby Checker. Her big break came in 1962 when her vocals were added to Chubby Checker's "Slow Twistin'," making it a duet. At 16, Sharp recorded "Mashed Potato Time" and became an overnight sensation.

Her many appearances on *American Bandstand* and at teen dances made her the first black female teenage idol in the early 1960s. In later years, Sharp did concert and club dates and became a very popular nightclub performer. Other charted singles: "Gravy," "Ride," "Do the Bird," "Wild," and "I Really Love You." Her later hits include "I'm Not in Love" (from the *Happy 'Bout the Whole Thing* album for which she wrote the title cut), "I'd Really Love to See You Tonight" (from the CD *What Color Is Love*), and "Breaking and Entering" and "I Love You Anyway" (from the CD *Dee Dee* produced by Jerry Butler).

She also appeared in Donald Byrd's *Nutcracker*, and in Billy Dee Williams' *Brown Sugar*. In recent years she has written commercials and been the spokesperson for "Shades of You" by Maybelline.

Web site: www.deedeesharp.com

GEORGIE SHAW

In the mid-1950s, Georgie Shaw won acclaim for a number of hits, among them, "Rags to Riches," "No Arms Can Ever Hold You," "Go On with the Wedding" (with Kitty Kallen), "Faded Summer Love," and "To You My Love."

BUNNY SIGLER

Bunny Sigler spent his formative years singing songs at Helping Hand Rescue Mission and also with several church groups. As a young man, he recorded for various local labels, besides singing and playing guitar and piano in area nightclubs. Leon Huff recommended Sigler to independent producers John Madara and Dave White, who signed him to a contract. When his first album, *Let the Good Times Roll & Feels So Good*, was released on Cameo-Parkway, the first single, "Girl Don't Make Me Wait," drew attention; and the title track (known first as a hit by Shirley and Lee) was a highly charted hit single in 1967 when Cameo-Parkway closed its doors.

Sigler later became a prolific songwriter–producer for Kenny Gamble and Leon Huff at Philadelphia International Records. His songs, productions, and piano and background vocals became an integral part of the company.

Other charted hits: "Let Me Party with You (Party, Party, Party)," "Tossin' and Turnin'," "You're So Fine" (a rework of the Falcons), "Lovey Dovey" (originally done by Clyde McPhatter), and "Only You." As a songwriter, Sigler wrote "Let Me Make Love to You" and "Your Body's Here with Me" (for the O'Jays) and cowrote such releases as "Sunshine" (O'Jays' follow-up to Backstabbers), "You Got Your Hooks in Me," "When the World Is at Peace," "Who Am I," and "Don't You Call Me Brother." (He has published over 300 songs.)

Among Sigler's LPs: *That's How Long I'll Be Loving You, Keep Smilin', My Music, Get Down on the Philly Jump,* and *I Got My Mind Made Up (You Can Get It Girl)*, produced for Instant Funk.

In the 1980s, Sigler continued to write and produce. "Somebody Loves You Baby" (cowritten with Eugene Curry) was a million-seller for Patti LaBelle, and "Do You Get Enough Love," a Number-1 R&B hit for Shirley Jones. In recent years, Sigler has collaborated on some of the final tracks of Phyllis Hyman, and also with Lou Rawls, Billy Paul, and Stephanie Mills.

Today, artists like Heavy D, Jay-Z, Kelly Rowland of Destiny's Child, Outkast, 7K, Fat Joe, 50 Cent, and new singer Lyfe have revived many Bunny Sigler songs, selling millions of copies.

Telephone: Conejo Productions, 215.983.6161

THE SILHOUETTES
Earl Beal, Raymond Edwards, Bill Horton, Rick Lewis

An R&B vocal harmony group, the Silhouettes scored big in 1957 with "Get a Job," considered by many to be *the* doo-wop song of the 1950s (written by group member Rick Lewis). They continued to perform through the 1960s with two of the four original members.

WILL SMITH

Will Smith began his career in the mid-'80s as the Fresh Prince, and by the '90s he became one of the biggest superstars of his time. After achieving success as a pop music artist, he starred in television and then a series of hit movies.

Born and raised in Philadelphia, Smith was originally offered a scholarship to MIT but chose to pursue a career in music. Some of his biggest hits: "Summertime," "Gettin' Jiggy with It," "Just the Two of Us," and "Miami." Several of his major box office hits: *Bad Boys, Men in Black,* and *Independence Day.*

THE SOUL SURVIVORS
Charlie Ingui, Richie Ingui, Ken Jeremiah, Joseph Furgione, Paul Venturini

Led by the Ingui brothers' soulful vocals, the Soul Survivors came to Philadelphia in the mid-'60s (from their native New York) and became a resident group. After a series of successful club and TV appearances, they were chosen to record "Expressway to Your Heart" on Crimson Records in 1967. It became the first national hit for producers Kenny Gamble and Leon Huff and a memorable song in R&B history. Popular recordings: "Explosion in My Soul," "Impossible Mission," and "City of Brotherly Love."

Web site: www.thesoulsurvivors.com

THE STYLISTICS
Russell Thompkins Jr., Airrion Love, James Smith, James Dunn, Herb Murrell

The Stylistics—Russell Thompkins Jr., Airrion Love, James Smith, James Dunn, and Herb Murrell—first got together in the late 1960s. With a unique sound and the pure falsetto of Thompkins, the Stylistics had a string of 12 Top-10 hits through the mid-1970s. Memorable songs: "You Make Me Feel Brand New," "I'm Stone in Love with You," "Break Up to Make Up," "People Make the World Go Round," "Betcha by Golly Wow," "Stop Look Listen (To Your Heart)," "You Are Everything," "You'll Never Get to Heaven," "Rockin' Roll Baby," "Can't Give You Anything," and "You're a Big Girl Now."

In the mid- to late '70s, the group enjoyed success in the U.K. Smith and Dunn left in the early '80s, and the three remaining Stylistics continued to tour well into the '90s.

In 2003, lead singer Thompkins formed a new group, Russell Thompkins Jr. and the New Stylistics, while remaining members Love and Murrell now bill themselves as the Stylistics.

TAMMI TERRELL

As a beautiful teen with gifted vocal ability, Tammi Terrell won a number of local talent contests and became the opening club act for performers such as Gary U.S. Bonds and Patti LaBelle and the Bluebelles. In the early 1960s, she made her recording debut with "If You See Bill," followed by "The Voice of Experience." Terrell later recorded "I Cried" for James Brown's Try Me label and toured with his revue. In 1965, at age 20, while performing with Jerry Butler in Detroit, she caught the attention of Berry Gordy Jr. and signed with Motown Records.

After cutting the R&B singles, "Come On and See Me," "This Old Heart of Mine," and "Hold Me Oh My Darling," Terrell was paired with Marvin Gaye. Together they created some of the greatest love songs ever to emerge from Motown. Their classic duets include "Ain't No Mountain High Enough," "Ain't Nothin' Like the Real Thing," and "You're All I Need to Get By." Tragically, she died at age 24, as the result of a brain tumor.

RUSSELL THOMPKINS JR.

For over 30 years, Russell Thompkins Jr. was the original lead singer of the Stylistics. His impeccable falsetto led the group to worldwide fame and success, notably seven gold albums, five gold singles, eight platinum albums, and four platinum singles. In 2000, he left the Stylistics, and, in 2002, recorded and released a solo album: *A Matter of Style* (in collaboration with Christopher Biehler of Forevermore Music and Records).

In 2003, he formed Russell Thompkins Jr. and the New Stylistics (with Raymond Johnson, James Ranton, and Jonathan Buckson), dedicated to preserving the sound of the original recordings.

Web site: www.russellthompkinsjr.com

THREE DEGREES
Fayette Pickney, Sheila Ferguson, Valerie Holiday, Helen Scott

In 1963, producer–songwriter Richard Barrett discovered the group, the Three Degrees, consisting of Fayette Pickney, Linda Turner, and Shirley Porter. Turner and Porter left and were replaced by Helen Scott and Janet Jones. In the mid-1960s, Sheila Ferguson and Valerie Holiday replaced Scott and Jones.

In 1970, the group had their first national hit with a remake of "Maybe" (a classic hit by the Chantels), with Helen Scott returning to do the lead vocals. The song reached Number 4, and their follow-up, "I Do Take You," reached Number 7.

After signing with Kenny Gamble and Leon Huff's Philadelphia International Records in 1973, Three Degrees had a disco hit called "Dirty Ol' Man." In 1974, they did the vocal track for "TSOP" (The Sound of Philadelphia), which was recorded by MFSB as the theme song for the TV show, *Soul Train*. Released as a single, it went gold and hit Number 1. That same year, they recorded "When Will I See You Again," which went platinum and sold over 2 million copies. Their follow-up, "I Didn't Know," was a big hit in 1975.

Fayette Pickney left the group about a year later, and Sheila Ferguson departed in 1986. Helen Scott (who returned again), Valerie Holiday, and Cynthia Garrison (a new member) recorded three albums in the '90s.

Web site: www.thethreedegrees.com

THE TRAMMPS
Jimmy Ellis (lead vocal), Harold Wade, Stanley Wade, Earl Young, Harold Watkins, Robert Upchurch, Ed Cermanski

In the 1970s, the Trammps emerged into the spotlight. Their first charted hit was "Zing Went the Strings of My Heart" (a revival of Judy Garland's 1940s tune). Other hits followed: "Hold Back the Night," "Where Do We Go From Here," and "Where the Happy People Go." In 1977, they scored with "Disco Inferno" (featured in the film, *Saturday Night Fever*), which won them a Grammy Award.

Web site: www.aaeg.com

THE TURBANS
Al Banks (lead vocal), Matthew Platt, Charles Williams, Andrew Jones

When the Turbans began performing in the mid-1950s, they recorded a song bass singer Andrew Jones had written, called "When You Dance," which became their biggest hit. Other charted singles: "Sister Sookey," "B-I-N-G-O," "It Was a Night like This," "Valley of Love," and "The Wadda-do."

THE TYMES
Donald Banks, Al "Caesar" Berry, Norman Burnett, George Hilliard, George Williams Jr.

The Tymes began singing in 1957 at record hops and local clubs. In 1963, they appeared on a WDAS Talent Show, *Tip Top Talent Hunt*, and were heard by an executive at Parkway.

A month later, they recorded a song written by George Williams, Roy Straigis, and Billy Jackson, called "So Much in Love," which became a Number-1 national hit. Other memorable songs: "Wonderful! Wonderful!," "Somewhere," "To Each His Own," "Here She Comes," and "People." Today, the original group, with new members Lafayette Gamble and Jimmy Wells, do concert dates all over the U.S.

Telephone: Letisse, Inc., 215.844.8374

VIRTUES
Frank Virtue (lead guitar), Jimmy Bruno (guitar), Ralph Frederico (piano), Barry Smith (drums)

Frank Virtue formed the group, Virtues, in the late 1940s. They played on radio and, by the mid-1950s, on TV. A song they recorded, called "Guitar Boogie Shuffle," became a hit in 1959.

CLARA WARD

Clara Ward became one of the greatest soloists in gospel history. With her backup group, the Ward Singers, she took gospel out of the church and into the nightclubs, singing pop gospel hits with glitz, glamour, and innovative arrangements of exceptional material.

Throughout the late '40s and '50s, they were gospel's elite, scoring many hits. In the '60s, Ward continued to tour (mostly the club circuit) with a revised group, playing Las Vegas and Disneyland.

GROVER WASHINGTON JR.

With his roots in R&B and soul–jazz organ combos, Grover Washington Jr. became a masterful musician and one of the most popular saxophonists of all time.

Washington began playing music at age 10 and, within a few years, began performing in clubs. He moved to Philadelphia in 1967 and recorded for the Prestige label (as a sideman). His first big seller was "Inner City Blues" in the early '70s. Becoming an important name after recording "Mister Magic" (1975), he solidified his status after compositions like "Winelight" (1980)

Washington later made many guest appearances on records, playing everything from pop to jazz. He died of a sudden heart attack in December 1999 at age 56.

ETHEL WATERS

Ethel Waters was an artist of great versatility, with an extended career as both a recording star and an actress on stage and screen. Born and raised just outside of Philadelphia (in nearby Chester), Waters began singing blues and jazz before making the transition to pop music star. She was a strong influence on the many vocalists that succeeded her. In later years, she played dramatic roles in feature films and then confined her performances to religious work.

▲ **Bobby Rydell** performs today, blending pop and past hits with a still-vibrant voice reminiscent of his earlier years. *Courtesy Ridarelli Family*

Chubby Checker, today, still in demand and performing to sold-out audiences nationwide. In the fall of 2005, he was presented with the Wildwood Music Award. At their Fabulous Fifties Weekend Concert, he gave a riveting performance before an enthusiastic crowd of 7,000 people. *Courtesy Twisted Entertainment*

▲ **Fabian** appears on the concert circuit and in past years has produced his own series of music specials (from the '50s and '60s), which have aired on public television and Pay Per View. *Courtesy Oscar Arslanian and Associates*

120

▲ **The Dovells,** with original members Mark Stevens, left, and Jerry Gross. Their current concert act is a skillful mix of music and comedy. *Courtesy Jerry Gross*

▲ **Dee Dee Sharp's** current repertoire includes contemporary R&B, jazz, and pop hits, plus her rock and soul favorites. *Courtesy Dee Dee Sharp*

▲ **The Orlons** Original members Stephen Caldwell and Jean Brickley Maddox lead a revised group that blends their charted hits with other songs of the era. *Courtesy Stephen Caldwell*

▲ **James Darren** After a lengthy career as an actor and director, he returned to performing, in 1999, recording for Concord Records, and appearing in concert. His recent CD *(Because of You)* is a tribute to many of our best-remembered pop vocalists. *Courtesy James Darren*

► **Frankie Avalon** continually tours in *Grease,* and with Fabian and Bobby Rydell, as well as with accomplished musician sons Frank (drums) and Anthony (guitar). *Courtesy Dina Avalon*

▲ **Lee Andrews** Blessed with a smooth and melodious voice, Andrews became one of the finest vocal talents ever to emerge from the City of Brotherly Love. *Photo: Weldon A. McDougal III*

▲ **The Tymes** *Left to right,* Norman Burnett, Lafayette Gamble, Donald Banks, Jimmy Wells, and Al "Caesar" Berry bring joy to countless fans, blending pop and R&B hits from the '60s and '70s. *Courtesy Al "Caesar" Berry*

▲ **Danny and the Juniors,** with, *left to right*, original members Frank Maffei and Joe Terry (the third member is Bob Maffei). They appear throughout the country and recently completed a tour of Italy. *Courtesy Frank Maffei*

▲ **Bobby Martin,** the awesome arranger and saxophonist. As Lawrence Brown said, "He could put horn lines together like you wouldn't imagine." *Photo: Weldon A. McDougal III*

▲ **Chubby Checker,** the music legend, *right,* presents Charlie Gracie with the Philadelphia Music Award for Lifetime Achievement in June of 2004. WOGL's Harvey Holiday holds the plaque as Joan Gracie looks on, *rear. Courtesy Charlie Gracie Jr.*

▲ **Kenny Gamble and Leon Huff** reunited with the **Soul Survivors** at the Philadelphia Music Alliance Awards in 1993. *Left to right,* Huff, Richie Ingui, Gamble, and Charlie Ingui. *Courtesy the Inguis*

▲ **The Original Comets,** on tour in the U.K. and still "rockin' around the clock." *Left to right,* Johnny Grande (keyboard), Dick Richards (drums), Marshall Lytle (bass), Jacko Buddin (guitar), Joey Ambrose (sax), Franny Beecher (guitar). *Courtesy Dick Richards*

▲ **Eddie Holman** today. His falsetto style of singing has earned him a unique place in soul music history. *Courtesy Sheila Holman*

▲ **Barbara Mason** entertains audiences from coast to coast and sounds better than ever. *Courtesy Marc Mason*

► **Bunny Sigler** is still active in today's music world, producing and consulting. Many of our recent artists have given new life to his songs, selling millions of copies. *Photo: Weldon A. McDougal III*

▲ **Russell Thompkins Jr. and the New Stylistics,** *left to right,* Russell Thompkins Jr., James Ranton, Raymond Johnson, Jonathan Buckson. Thompkins continues to impress audiences with his gifted vocal ability. At his 2005 induction into the Vocal Group Harmony Hall of Fame, his performance of "Betcha by Golly Wow" received a standing ovation. *Courtesy Florence Thompkins*

▲ **Billy Paul** recently completed international tours of Europe and South America and continues to record. *Courtesy Blanche Williams*

▲ **Sigma Sound's** beat goes on for fathers and sons in the late '90s. Left to right, *standing*, Joe Tarsia and Eddie Lavert; *seated*, Gerald Lavert and Michael Tarsia. *Courtesy Joe Tarsia*

▲ **Kenny Gamble,** *left,* greets former **Soul Survivor Ken Jeremiah** at the TSOP Lounge in Atlantic City in the spring of 2005. *Courtesy Lew Steiner/Atlantic City Weekly*

▲ **William Hart's** recent work includes his latest CD, *360 Degrees of the Delfonics,* released on La La Records, which blends today's beat with Hart's style of singing. *Photo: Weldon A. McDougal III*

▲ **The Soul Survivors,** Charlie Ingui, left, and Richie Ingui, perform at the World Trade Center on July 11, 2001. They became one of the finer blue-eyed soul groups in R&B history. *Courtesy Lila Ingui*

129

▲ **The Original Blue Notes** (formerly of Harold Melvin and the Blue Notes), *clockwise from top,* Lloyd Parks, Lawrence Brown, Arthur Aikens, Lenny ("Mr. Unforgettable") Edwards, and Dr. Salaam Love, *center. Courtesy the Original Blue Notes*

▲ **Patti LaBelle,** still vivacious and stunning, continues to enjoy a long-lasting career in contemporary music. *Courtesy W&W Public Relations*

▲ **Richard Barrett** became one of our most successful independent record producers, and also a pioneering producer on Broadway. *Photo: Weldon A. McDougal III*

▲ **Purple Reign** today, *left to right, front row,* Paul Beato, Nevis Truitt, Johnny Greco; *back row,* Bob Gonnella, Joe Fox, Bob Beato, Norman Guarni, Joe Mariani. *Courtesy Bob Beato*

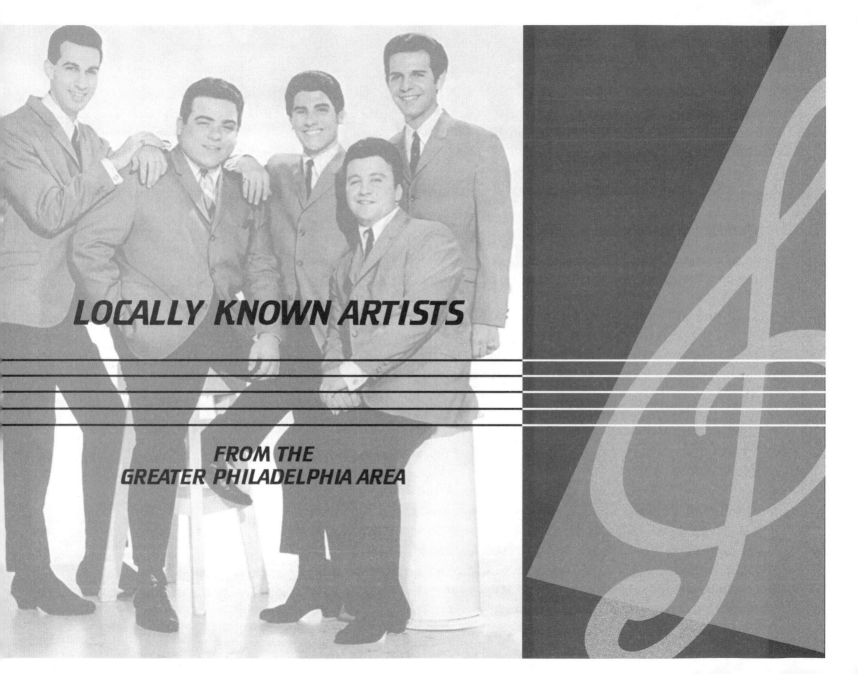

LOCALLY KNOWN ARTISTS

FROM THE
GREATER PHILADELPHIA AREA

AMBASSADORS

The Ambassadors reached the R&B charts, in 1969, with the soul-style ballad, "I Really Love You," cowritten by Kenny Gamble. Subsequently, they released the album, *Soul Summit,* which features Leon Huff on piano and Earl Young on drums.

ANTHONY AND THE SOPHOMORES
Anthony Maresco (lead vocal), Ernie Funaro (first tenor), Richie Benatti (second tenor) Johnny Donato (second tenor), Anthony Perri (baritone), Bobby Beato (bass)

Anthony and the Sophomores' greatest hits came, in 1963, with "Play Those Oldies Mr. D.J." (written by members of the 4 J's) and, in 1965, when they recorded "Gee, but I'd Give the World" (affectionately known as "Gee") on ABC Paramount (produced by Joe Terry of Danny and the Juniors). Other hits: "Get Back to You" (on ABC Paramount) and "Serenade" (on Jamie-Guyden).

GEORGE "BUTCH" BALLARD

George "Butch" Ballard became a renowned drummer and provided rhythm for various jazz greats. He began to work professionally in the early 1940s, first playing with Fats Waller. In the mid-'40s, Ballard worked with Louis Armstrong and, later, with Eddie "Lockjaw" Davis. He performed with Duke Ellington on a European tour in 1950 and then played with the Count Basie band. Returning to Philadelphia in 1954, Ballard performed with such jazz stars as Dinah Washington and Nina Simone. For many years, he toured throughout Europe with trumpeter Clark Terry. Ballard later became a popular and inspirational drum instructor and, in recent times, has performed with the Philadelphia Legends of Jazz Orchestra.

BILLY AND THE ESSENTIALS
Billy Carlucci (lead vocal), Mike Lenihan, John Caulfield, Peter Torres, Phil D'Antonio

Beginning as a group in Southwest Philly, Billy and the Essentials recorded "The Dance Is Over" for Madara/White in 1960. Other hit songs: "Maybe You'll Be There," "Over the Weekend," "Babalu's Wedding Day," "Young at Heart," and "Don't Cry (Sing Along with the Music)."

Billy Carlucci also recorded several hits with Dawn, including "Let's Get Together" and "O'Wee Baby" (both written by Carlucci's then partner, Leon Huff) on Mercury Records. (Carlucci is also an accomplished songwriter with a resume of over 600 songs.) He later sang with Danny and the Juniors in the '70s and '80s.

JERRY BLAVAT

Jerry Blavat began his musical internship as the top male dancer on *Bob Horn's Bandstand* from 1953 to 1956. After graduating from high school in 1958, he began promoting records for Cameo-Parkway and was road manager for Danny and the Juniors.

In 1960, Blavat got into radio by an act of bravado. The owner of the Venus Lounge in Philadelphia bet "the Geator with the Heater" he could not do a radio show from his nightclub. So Blavat went to WCAM in Camden and purchased an hour of radio time, with the right to resell the commercials within it. Blavat proceeded to do just that, to pay for the airtime. When a severe snowstorm closed the club, and the city, too, Blavat made his way to WCAM, determined to air those commercials and armed with an assortment of Chuck Berry, Fats Domino, and Little Richard records few teens had heard at the time. The storm that immobilized the listeners also immobilized the Geator's replacements at the station. So, his one hour of evening radio time turned into an all-nighter.

Unlike other D.J.s, Blavat provided informative commentary on the music he played and the artists who performed it. Listeners didn't know which was better, his patter or his platters. He continued the frenetic pace until the morning D.J. showed up at 6 A.M. By then, the verdict was in. Blavat was a huge hit and began a career that has never lost momentum.

In addition to his radio and TV work over the past 44 years, "the Boss with the Hot Sauce" has appeared at dances, clubs, and events all over the Delaware Valley and "down the shore" (including his summer residence at Memories, his dance club), introducing several generations to the sound he's made the musical signature of Philadelphia.

TIMMY BROWN

Timmy Brown began as an all-pro running back in the 1960s NFL with the Philadelphia Eagles, but his heart was in music.

As a child growing up in an Indiana orphanage, Brown studied voice and tap. In college, he formed his own band and performed at clubs and dances.

In the early '60s, in Philadelphia, Brown studied voice with Artie Singer and recorded for the Singular and Mercury labels. After releases of "Running Late" and "If I Loved You," he scored with "I've Got a Secret," which rose on the local charts.

He later turned to acting and appeared in such feature films as *Mash* and *Nashville*. On TV, he played the role of Spearchucker in the early years of *Mash*, and was a regular on the soap opera, *Capitol*. He also guest-starred in *T. J. Hooker, Nell, The Mary Tyler Moore Show, Adam-12, Cades County*, and *The Wild, Wild West*.

JONATHAN P. CASEY

While serving in the U.S. Navy during the Vietnam War, Jonathan P. Casey first became program director for armed forces radio station WBEL.

In 1972, he joined WSNJ AM and FM as afternoon host and was later named the station's musical director. Casey hosted a late afternoon show, in the late '70s, on WDVL FM. He left radio for a number of years to pursue a corporate management career. In 1994, Casey returned to WSNJ Radio as music director and afternoon host.

DANNY CEDRONE

Danny Cedrone is known for his legendary work as the lead guitarist for Billy Haley and His Comets on such hits as "Rock around the Clock," "Shake Rattle and Roll," and "Rock the Joint." Cedrone's memorable guitar solos galvanized the rock 'n' roll audience as no other had before and resonated with millions of listeners all over the world. Unfortunately, he died prematurely as the result of a tragic accident, unaware of how far-reaching his work would become and how great its impact would be. One of the all-time great guitarists.

LOU COSTELLO

Known as the "Dancing D.J." to his many fans throughout the tristate area, Lou Costello has been playing blues, R&B, and street-corner harmony along with dance tunes of the '60s and '70s for over 30 years. In addition to being heard daily and every Wednesday night (as host of the *Doo-Wop Diner*) on WVLT 92.1 FM, Costello has become a popular

host of countless local rock 'n' rolls shows and is proud to call many of the performers his friends.

THE EPSILONS
Gene McFadden, John Whitehead, Allen Beatty, Lloyd Parks, James Knight

The Epsilons began as a teenage group and got their first break when they toured with Otis Redding. They also did the background vocals for Arthur Conley (a one-time member of the group) on his hit, "Sweet Soul Music." Their initial release came out on Stax Records. Lloyd Parks left the group and joined Broadway Express (later becoming a member of Harold Melvin and the Blue Notes.)

McFadden and Whitehead renamed the Epsilons Talk of the Town, and the group recorded several singles for North Bay Records. In 1973, they joined Kenny Gamble and became involved with songwriting and producing and the group eventually disbanded.

(*See* McFadden and Whitehead)

THE ETHICS
Ron Tyson, Joe Freeman, Carl Enlow, Andrew Collins

The Ethics first came together in 1967, led by Ron Tyson, who was recognized as an exceptional vocalist and songwriter. Their local hits include "Sad, Sad Story" and "Think about Tomorrow." In 1969, the group had two R&B charted songs: "Farewell" and "Tell Me." The Ethics disbanded in the early 1970s.

THE EXCEPTIONS
Jimmy Ellis, Earl Young, Val Walker, Russell Boston, Charles Hynes

The Exceptions' first release in 1965 was "Down by the Ocean," which created attention locally and was later picked up by Cameo Records. A later effort, entitled "A Sad Goodbye," was released on Parkway Records. Jimmy Ellis and Earl Young became members of the Trammps in the early '70s.

FABULOUS FOUR (FOUR J'S)
Jr. Pirollo (lead vocal), Jimmy Testa (tenor), Ernie Spano (baritone), Joe Milaro (baritone), Bob Finizio (bass)

Known early in their career as the Four J's, the group later became the Fabulous Four, when they traveled with Fabian. In the mid-'60s, they resurfaced as the Four J's (also referred to as the 4 J's).

Buddy Greco discovered the group in 1957 after they won a contest at Sons of Italy Purple Astor Lounge in South Philadelphia. Within a few months, they released "Rock and Roll Age," which became their first charted hit. Later successes include "By Love Possessed," "Here I am Broken Hearted," and a covered version of "Dreamin'." The group wrote the songs, "Play Those Oldies Mr. D.J.," "Walk On with

the Duke" (Gene Chandler's follow-up to "Duke of Earl"), and "Wild Party." Along with Anthony and the Sophomores, and Billy and the Essentials, they were a beloved local group in the city of Philadelphia.

FOUR EPICS
Jack "Rocky" McKnight, Mickey Neal, Jimmy Mullen, Richard Lalli

The Four Epics' recordings include "Again," "Cupid," and "I'm on My Way to Love" (in 1962, for Jerry Ross on Heritage Records).

FREDDY BELL AND THE BELLBOYS
A very popular local group in the mid-'50s, Freddy Bell and the Bellboys had a Top-10 hit in England with "Gitty-up-a-Ding-Dong" in 1956. That same year, Elvis Presley saw them performing Willie Mae Thornton's "Hound Dog" and decided to record it himself. The group also appeared in the movie, *Rock around the Clock*.

THE FUTURES
Frank Washington, Kenny Crew, James King, John King, Henry McGilberry

The Futures first recorded for Kenny Gamble and Leon Huff (on the Gamble label) with "Love Is Here." After a series of singles released by Buddah Records, they rejoined Gamble and Huff on Philadelphia International Records in 1978.

Their most successful recording was "Part Time Party Time Man," succeeded by "Ain't No Time for Nothing" and "Mr. Bojangles." They also did two albums: *Past, Present and the Futures*, and *Greetings of Peace*.

RICHIE GRASSO

Richie Grasso has long been involved with many groups, including the Five Classics, the Styles, and Billy and the Essentials (he sang bass on "Babalu's Wedding Day"). Grasso was also a member of the Tokens for many years. As a songwriter, he's penned songs for the Righteous Brothers, Brook Benton, Oliver, the Three Degrees, Jackie DeShannon, and Peter and Gordon. Hits include "Do Unto Me" and "I Can Remember." Grasso also cowrote the Top-10 '60s hit "Sweet Cherry Wine" (with Tommy James).

MAUREEN GRAY

Maureen Gray began singing at age three and performed solo in a children's program at Carnegie Hall at age five. Discovered by John Madara at age twelve, she went on to record and achieve success with regional hits, such as "Today's the Day," "Crazy over You," "I Don't Want to Cry," and "Dancing the Strand."

JOHNNY GRECO

In 1962, Johnny Greco's recording of "Rocket Ride" became a local favorite. The song was written by Dave Appell and released on a subsidiary label of Cameo-Parkway. Greco later formed a band (Hot Ice), which performed progressive rock, and, in the late '60s, he became the lead singer of the Four Epics. Until recently, he was a member of Purple Reign.

JERRY GREENE

In 1960, Brooklyn native Jerry Greene created Lost Nite Records, which released the hit, "There's a Moon Out Tonight," by the Capris. He came to Philadelphia in 1961 and opened the Record Museum, a retail store specializing in oldies. (Eventually there were 25 stores in the Greater Philadelphia Area.) In 1962, Greene cocreated Crimson Records, a label that produced such groups as Lee Andrews and the Hearts, the Masters (with member John Oates), and the Soul Survivors. He launched Collectables Records and Gotham Distributing (with wife Nina) in 1980, and Alpha Video, in 2002, to release vintage films and television shows.

ALI HACKETT ("KING OF THE OLDIES")

Growing up in nearby Chester, Ali Hackett began singing with the Twilights and TNJ's. He began his radio career in 1974 on WTNJ in Trenton, where he hosted a top-rated show for three years. He later was an on-air personality at WHAT in Philadelphia (for 12 years), where he played R&B; made commercials; read news, weather, and sports; interviewed guests; and emceed live shows. In 2005, Hackett hosted a weekly show on WVLT 92.1 FM.

BILLY HARNER

Billy Harner grew up in the South Jersey area and began recording in the early '60s. His local and regional late '60s hits include "Sally Sayin' Somethin'," "Homicide Dresser," and "She's Almost You." In the early '70s, he recorded "What about the Children," released by Bell Records.

DOUGLAS "JOCKO" HENDERSON ("YOUR ACE FROM OUTER SPACE")

Said to have had one of the most unique and pleasant voices in the broadcasting industry, Douglas "Jocko" Henderson began his career at WBAL in Baltimore, and then came to WHAT in Philadelphia. Later moving to WDAS, he was, at one time, on the air in both Philly and New York. In 1970, Henderson started a local magazine called *Philly Talk* and also produced and promoted records. In later years, he spent time promoting his *Get Ready* program—in which he recorded himself teaching everything from math to American history, with rap lyrics—for school districts around the country.

HONEY AND THE BEES
Nadine Felder, Jean Davis, Gwendolyn Oliver, Cassandra "Ann" Wooten

Coming together in the late '60s, Honey and the Bees were a female soul quartet backed by members of the Gamble–Huff organization. The group toured local clubs in Philadelphia and along the East Coast until1973, when they stopped performing.

JEREMIAH HUNTER

The high-energy band, Jeremiah Hunter (led by ex–Soul Survivor Ken Jeremiah), plays many high-profile events throughout the East Coast. Jeremiah also leads Impulse, a party dance band, which includes Grammy Award–winning guitarist Tony Davilio (the music arranger on John Lennon's *Double Fantasy* album).

Web site: www.kennyjeremiah.com

ED HURST

Born and raised in Atlantic City, Ed Hurst originated the *950 Club* with partner Joe Grady on WPEN in postwar Philadelphia. It was the first teenage dance show on the air. In the early 1950s, Hurst moved his show to TV and was broadcast every Saturday. Grady and Hurst had a daily TV show from Wilmington in the mid-1950s that rivaled *Bandstand*. In 1960, their *Summertime on the Pier* began airing on WRCV-TV and became a fixture every summer weekend for nearly two decades.

Hurst returned to WPEN, in the 1980s, with partner Joe Grady to host the *950 Club*. When Grady retired in 1987, Ed Hurst remained on the air almost 50 years after it all began.

KING ARTHUR

A South Philly kid, King Arthur began in the late '60s doing local record hops and hosting a weekend radio show on WCAM in Camden, New Jersey. He later moved to TV, where he hosted the South Philadelphia Talent Workshop, and appeared as the "Fan Man" on KYW-TV3 with Ron Luck.

Today, *King Arthur's Crown Sounds* is heard every Friday night, Saturday afternoon, and Sunday evening on WNJC 1360 AM (Philadelphia's Renaissance Radio Station). In addition, the King is heard every Sunday night on the Web.

Web site:www.destinationdoowop.com

KIT KATS
**John Bradley (lead vocal), Karl Hausman (keyboard),
Kit Stewart (drummer)**

The Kit Kats formed in 1962 and hit their stride later, in the mid-to-late '60s, becoming a very popular attraction in the Philadelphia area. The group's repertoire, with songs written by Karl Hausman and Kit Stewart, was a mixture of doo-wop, '50s and '60s rock, pop, and soul. Playing their own instruments, they produced harmonies that surpassed the quality of the major groups of the day. "That's the Way" and "Let's Get Lost on a Country Road" were big local hits for the Kit Kats in 1966. They changed their name to New Hope in 1969, and, that same year, recorded "Won't Find Better than Me," which reached 57 on the national charts. The group disbanded in 1974.

STEVE KURTZ

Steve Kurtz grew up in the music industry—his father started Galax-Z Records—and managed a late '50s doo-wop group (Farrel and the Flames). In 1976, Kurtz created his own entertainment business, providing live bands and sound systems for a variety of events. In the '80s, he emceed a local cable TV variety show and, in the '90s, originated the Steve Kurtz Show on radio. Since 2001, he has hosted a weekly show on WVLT FM, featuring the oldies. Kurtz is also heard on the Internet (playing obscure doo-wop) and was recently given the Destry Award for Best Show Host and Excellence in Broadcasting. For the last five years, he has hosted an anniversary show from Cleveland's Rock and Roll Hall of Fame, broadcast back to the Delaware Valley.

THE LARKS

The Larks, a very popular '60s soul group in Philadelphia, helped to provide a transition from the days of doo-wop to the smoother era of soul. Besides singing bass, Weldon McDougal III, the dynamo of the group, also wrote and produced for the Larks. Initially, their lead singer was Jackie Marshall, followed by Cleopatra McDougal (Weldon's first wife) and, later, by Vivian McDougal (Weldon's second wife). (*See* Weldon Arthur McDougal III)

HY LIT

Considered the voice of Philadelphia radio over the past 50 years, Hy Lit ("Hyski-Orooni-McVouty-Ozoot") has been taking his listeners uptown, downtown, and crosstown. A pioneer of rock 'n' roll radio, Lit became a Philadelphia phenomenon on WIBG (99 AM) during his nightly 6 to 10 P.M. shift. He later had his own television show.

Lit's popularity kept him in demand at dance halls and clubs across the Delaware Valley. In the 1970s, he served as master of ceremonies for the Harlem Globetrotters all across the country. In recent years, Lit was in residence at WOGL (98.1 FM) playing the oldies. Currently, he can be heard on the Web.

Web site: www.hylitradio.com

LITTLE JOE AND THE THRILLERS
Joe Cook (lead vocal), Harry Pascle, Farris Hill, Donald Burnett, Richard Frazier

In 1957, Joe Cook and his group, Little Joe and the Thrillers, recorded a song he had written, called "Peanuts," which became a national hit on Okeh Records.

LITTLE JOEY AND THE FLIPS
Joey Hall, Jeff Leonard, Jimmy Meagher, John Smith, Freddy Gerace

The biggest hit for Little Joey and the Flips was "Bongo Stomp," which reached Number 23 on the pop charts in the summer of '62. Other songs: "It Was like Heaven" and "Fool, Fool, Fool."

JOHNNY MADARA

Johnny Madara has been a producer, composer, and vocalist. In 1957, he recorded "Be My Girl" (written by his vocal coach Artie Singer), which made the national charts. His other charted songs include "Heavenly" and "Vacation Time." Madara also recorded the song, "Do the Bop" (cowritten with Dave White), which was later retitled, rewritten, and released by Artie Singer (on his Singular Records label) as "At the Hop", a Number-1 national hit by Danny and the Juniors. In addition to producing local artists in the early to mid-'60s, Madara and White wrote such hits as "The Fly" (Chubby Checker), "1-2-3" (Len Barry), and "You Don't Own Me" (Leslie Gore).

(*See* the Spokesmen)

BOB MARCUCCI

Bob Marcucci began writing songs with his friend Pete DeAngelis after graduating from South Philadelphia High School. After shopping their demos to various record labels, Marcucci and DeAngelis formed their own company, naming their label Chancellor (after the Chancellor Hotel, where Marcucci's brother managed the dining room). In 1957, lightning struck when the talented duo wrote and produced a song, "With All My Heart," recorded by Jodie Sands, which became a national hit.

With the success of Jodie Sands, Marcucci decided to develop and manage talent, along with promoting records that he and DeAngelis wrote and produced. Subsequently, Marcucci discovered Frankie Avalon and Fabian Forte, who became national stars and moved to California in the early '60s to pursue their respective movie careers. In 1964, with their success in Hollywood on the rise, and the style of music changing, they and Marcucci ended their professional association.

In 1979, Marcucci began working as a technical advisor on a feature film called *The Idolmaker*. This experience led Marcucci to produce the remake of two classic 20th Century Fox films from the 1940s: *Razor's Edge* (released theatrically), and *A Letter to Three Wives* (an NBC Movie of the Week).

Today, Marcucci is still active (as president of Chancellor Entertainment) in California, writing his autobiography and developing film projects.

TOMMY MCCARTHY

A native of South Jersey, Tommy McCarthy began his career in 1975 at various radio stations, such as WCAM in Camden and WMID in Atlantic City. In 1982, he began broadcasting on WSNI/WPGR in Philadelphia with Hy Lit and, since 1993, has been the music director of WOGL FM. He received two nominations for Achievement in Radio Awards, in 1997, and is a five-time nominee for the Best Overnight Host. In 2004, McCarthy began hosting a Saturday night TV show on the QBC TV2 Cable Network.

WELDON ARTHUR MCDOUGAL III

Raised in the Richard Allen projects of North Philadelphia, Weldon Arthur McDougal III later became involved in music with classmates George Tindley (of the Dreams) and George Grant (of the Castelles). He has enjoyed a lengthy career in music (since the 1950s) as a recording artist, songwriter, producer, promotions representative, and photographer.

In the mid-1960s, McDougal co-owned Harthon Records and produced such artists as Eddie Holman, Barbara Mason, the Tiffanys, the Twilights, Herb Ward, Joanne Jackson, the Larks, and the Volcanos.

As the first black promotional representative to work for a major Philadelphia distributor (Chips), he was assigned to promote Motown Records. After his stint with Motown, Philadelphia International Records employed McDougal as director of special projects; he worked in South America with Archie Bell and the Drells, in Africa with Bunny Sigler and Instant Funk, and in Japan with the Three Degrees.

His photography credits include two books: *The Michael Jackson Scrapbook: The Early Days of the Jackson Five* (Avon Books, 1985) and *Motown: The Golden Years* (KP Books, 2001).

LEON MITCHELL

Leon Mitchell became a premiere alto sax player in Philadelphia and, very early on, focused on composition and arrangement. In the '60s, he became the A & R (artists and repertoire) director for Blue Note Records, supervising sessions for many noted jazz musicians. Max Roach later recorded his musical tribute to Billy Holiday. From 1964 to 1974, Mitchell was house bandleader for the Uptown Theater, where he worked with everyone who was anyone in R&B. One of his greatest hits during the Beatlemania period was "Boogaloo Down Broadway," recorded by the "fantastic Johnny C." (It reached Number 2 on the pop charts.)

Among Mitchell's notable arrangement students are Philly arrangers–writers–producers Thom Bell, Norman Harris, Ron Kersey, and noted vocalist Donny Hathaway (who received his first lesson from Mitchell). In later years, Mitchell became the musical director of the Philadelphia Legends of Jazz Orchestra, a position he holds to this day.

JIM NETTLETON

Jim Nettleton has enjoyed a lengthy career in radio and television (spanning 46 years) as an on-air performer, writer, producer, and program director. He began his career in Pottstown, Pennsylvania, in 1958, and subsequently worked in Connecticut at WDRC (Hartford) and WAVZ (New Haven). In 1970, Nettleton formed Cantour Productions, one of the early long-form syndicators of radio specials to the industry.

His affiliation with Philadelphia began in the mid-'60s as part of WFIL's original staff, which took "Boss Radio" to Number 1 in town and made the station the prototype Top-40 model in the country.

Nettleton later became director of programming and operations for WCAU (now WOGL) FM's oldies format and, in 1974, received *Billboard* magazine's Program Director of the Year award. In the early '80s, he originated, produced, and hosted the highly successful Saturday night *Big Band Show* on WPEN.

Nettleton later spent nine years in Tampa, Florida, as vice president of operations for WDAE and as the voice of channels 8 and 10. Returning to Philadelphia in 1993, he was affiliated with WOGL for the remainder of the decade, contributing to both specialty weekend programs on Saturday and the Sunday *Countdown Show*.

A two-time winner of the Best Weekend Show (Philadelphia Air Awards), Nettleton hosted the late-afternoon Oldies Show on WPEN from 2004 to 2005.

JOE NIAGARA ("THE ROCKIN' BIRD")

As a South Philadelphia youth, Joe Niagara grew up wanting to be a radio announcer. Discharged from the service at age 19, he began working on WDAS in 1947. After filing records at the station, Niagara's wish came true when he was given the chance to introduce some records on the air. Two years later, he landed a job at WIBG and remained there for 10 years.

In the late 1950s, Niagara was one of the top rock 'n' roll D.J.s in Philadelphia. After a three-year stint at KBIG in Los Angeles, he returned to WIBG and remained there through the 1960s. In the mid-1970s, he came to WPEN and remained on the air for 25 years.

BOB PANTANO

As the host of the popular *Saturday Night Dance Party* (simulcast on WOGL in Philadelphia and on 94.3 in Wildwood and the Jersey Shore), Bob Pantano has pioneered a show that has become the nation's longest-running radio dance program.

Born and raised in South Philadelphia, Pantano began spinning at record hops in the late '60s and then moved to nightclubs in the '70s, where he entertained and engaged audiences with upbeat dance music. He currently hosts the weekly TV show *Happenings*, which airs on various Comcast cable outlets in the Philadelphia and South Jersey areas.

Pantano keeps the concert circuit hopping with his well-known *Sounds of Philly* show, featuring some of the best local and national recording artists. He has hosted shows at the Wachovia Center, Tweeter Center, Penn's Landing, Trump Plaza, Resorts Casino, Wildwood Convention Center, and summer concerts in Philadelphia and South Jersey parks.

As a member of the board of directors of Variety Club, Pantano works to help children with disabilities.

Web site: www.bobpantano.com

PATTI AND THE EMBLEMS
Patti Russell (lead vocal)

Patti and the Emblems reached Number 37 on the national charts in 1964 with "Mixed-Up Shook-Up Girl" (cowritten by Leon Huff and Bill Carlucci).

PHILLY DEVOTIONS
Mathew Covington (lead vocal), Ernest Gibson (second tenor), Morris Taylor (baritone), Ellis Hill (bass)

Recording from the early to late '70s, the Philly Devotions scored with some of their local hits: "I Just Can't Say Goodbye," "I'll Never Color You a Rainbow," and "Hurt So Bad (Part 2)."

THE PREMIERS
Joe Mozoff, Lew Gaudioso, Al Waldman, John DePalma

The Premiers' releases include "False Love" and "Tonight" (one of the first recordings on Parkway).

DEAN RANDOLPH

Dean Randolph recorded songs on Chancellor, MGM, ABC Paramount, and APT Records, with such local hits and popular releases as "False Love," "How about That," "Fair Weather Friends," "Lonely Eyes," "Stay Away from Mary," and "Girl in the White Convertible."

RICK AND THE MASTERS
Anthony Trombetta (lead vocal), Frankie Condo, Richie Fininzio, Mike Silenzio

Some of the memorable releases by Rick and the Masters include "Bewitched, Bothered and Bewildered," "Let It Please Be You," "Flame of Love," and "I Don't Want Your Love."

JERRY ROSS

As the owner of Heritage and Colossus Records in the mid- to late '60s, Jerry Ross produced such groups as the Dreamlovers, Spanky and Our Gang, Jay and the Techniques, and Keith. He also cowrote (with Kenny Gamble and Leon Huff) "I'm Gonna Make You Love Me," which was subsequently recorded by Dee Dee Warwick, Madeline Bell, and Diana Ross/Temptations, and "You Gave Me Somebody to Love," sung by the Dreamlovers and later covered by Purple Reign.

KENNY ROSSI

Kenny Rossi became known to a national audience as a featured dancer on Dick Clark's *American Bandstand*, and, at the height of his popularity, left the show to pursue a recording career. By the early '60s, he became an accomplished vocalist recording on Roulette and later Mercury Records, with such local and regional hits as "But I Do," "I'll Never Smile Again," and "She Loves Me, She Loves Me Not." Rossi continued to perform through the 1960s, touring with Dick Clark's *Caravan of Stars* and doing club and concert dates. He ended his career in 1973 and went into private business.

SOLOMON "KAL" RUDMAN

As the publisher of *Friday Morning Quarterback*, six national music trade publications, Solomon "Kal" Rudman tracked the play rotations of pop songs broadcast over the air waves at major market stations and predicted which new songs to watch. Each magazine focused on a different genre of music.

Initially a science teacher in the Bristol Township school system, Rudman began his broadcasting career as a Top-40 radio jock on WCAM and later moved to WDAS. In the mid-'60s, he became the first R&B editor at *Billboard* magazine. He created his first trade magazine, in 1968, and continued to do syndicated broadcasts.

In the early '80s, Rudman appeared on many Merv Griffin music specials and also as the resident music expert on NBC's *Today* show. He served as an announcer, in the mid-'80s, for the World Wrestling Federation.

Rudman (along with his wife Lucille) are also noted philanthropists (particularly interested in education and public safety) and are very active in charity work.

CINDY SCOTT

Cindy Scott began singing at age 14 with sister Lynda and later with the Ordettes (which included Patti LaBelle). In 1967, she had two releases on Veep Records (for producers John Madara and Dave White): "I Love You Baby" and Otis Redding's "I've Been Loving You Too Long."

THE SHERRYS

Joe Cook, who was the lead singer of Little Joe and the Thrillers, formed the singing group the Sherrys, which consisted of his two daughters and two of their friends. The girls recorded two hits in the early 1960s: "Pop, Pop Pop-Pie" and "Slop Time."

ARTIE SINGER

As a musician, bandleader, songwriter, and voice teacher, Artie Singer was instrumental in developing the talents of Al Martino, James Darren, Chubby Checker, Bobby Rydell, and Dee Dee Sharp. In recent times, he has composed and presented a Broadway musical, with lyrics by Marjorie Baderak and libretto by Lisa and Sherry Gresson, and collaborated with Ray Straigis on a new PAX TV children's series: *Gina D's Kids Club*.

SHIRLEY SLAUGHTER

A native Philadelphian, Shirley Slaughter became an acclaimed songstress in the United Kingdom, with "Real Love" her biggest charted hit there. Currently, she tours throughout the U.S. and has appeared with the Funk Brothers.

THE SPOKESMEN
John Madara (lead vocal), Dave White, Ray Gilmore

John Madara and Dave White (formerly of Danny and the Juniors) formed the Spokesmen in the mid-'60s. They released "The Dawn of Correction," which became an answer to the hit song, "Eve of Destruction," by Barry McGuire (a protest song that portrayed a bleak picture of the future during a period of unrest in America). "The Dawn of Correction" gave a more positive view but became very controversial. Nevertheless, the song was a huge success and reached the Top 20 on the charts. The group also had local hits with "Michelle" and "I Love How You Love Me."

CHRISTY SPRINGFIELD

Christy Springfield began her career in Atlantic City at WMID AM and later worked at WAYV (the Number-1 station in the market). In 1983, she came to Philadelphia and began doing the overnight shift on Hot Hits 98 WCAU FM. Springfield also served as frequent host on USA Network's *Dance Party USA*.

As 98 WCAU FM changed to WOGL and an oldies format, in 1987, Springfield made the transition to late night, as host of the immensely popular *Backseat Memories*. In the spring of 2000, she switched to mid-day.

After 23 years at WOGL, in 2005, Springfield went to Oldies 950 WPEN, where she hosted the mid-day slot as well. When WPEN changed to a sports-talk format, she remained with the Greater Philadelphia Radio Group to do voice-over work and special projects for WPEN, WMGK, WMMR, and WBEN FM.

MARY SWAN

Blessed with great vocal quality, Mary Swan recorded on Swan Records in the 1950s, recording, among other hits, "My Heart Belongs to Only You" and "My Girlfriend Betty."

THE SWEETHEARTS OF SIGMA SOUND
Barbara Ingram, Evette Benton, Carla Benson

When Thom Bell recruited them, Barbara Ingram, Evette Benton, and Carla Benson were Camden natives and music majors at Glassboro State College. Throughout the 1970s, they sang background on all of the hit records produced by Bell and others for such artists as the Stylistics, Spinners, O'Jays, and Harold Melvin and the Blue Notes, to name a few.

JOSEPH "BUTTERBALL" TAMBURRO

Joseph "Butterball" Tamburro has enjoyed a 41-year career with WDAS radio in Philadelphia as a programmer, manager, on-air personality, and Rock 'n' Roll Hall of Fame nominee. His managerial skills and programming influence span markets across the country and have brought him national acclaim. Locally, Tamburro has been honored for community excellence and service by several mayors, the NAACP, the FBI, and the American Jewish Committee. In 2005, he was given the Lifetime Achievement Award from Clear Channel Radio.

JOE TARSIA

As chief engineer at Cameo-Parkway and later as owner–operator of Sigma Studios, Joe Tarsia recorded most of the music made in both the rock 'n' roll and Philly soul era. After Cameo-Parkway closed its doors in 1967, Tarsia hocked his house, car, and everything he owned to lease the second floor of 212 North 12th Street in Center City. He built Sigma's first studio wire by wire and knob by knob. On August 5, 1968, Sigma opened its doors, with limited funds and no staff. Tarsia booked and engineered the sessions, fixed the equipment, and cleaned the studio. In just months, Sigma added staff and began to operate around the clock.

Innovations under Tarsia brought Sigma to the cutting edge of sound recording. It became the first studio to offer console automation and one of the first to offer multitrack noise reduction.

The success of Sigma regulars—Kenny Gamble and Leon Huff; Thom Bell; Bobby Martin; and Ron Baker, Norman Harris, and Earl Young—attracted a string of top artists and producers from around the world. Some of the many artists Tarsia recorded include Bobby Rydell, Chubby Checker, Dee Dee Sharp, the Orlons, the Dovells, the Tymes, the Soul Survivors, the Intruders, Jerry Butler, Dusty Springfield, the Delfonics, the Stylistics, the O'Jays, the Spinners, Billy Paul, Harold Melvin and the Blue Notes, Lou Rawls, the Jacksons, Patti LaBelle, Teddy Pendergrass, and Stevie Wonder.

UNFORGETTABLE

Lenny Edwards (currently a member of Harold Melvin's Original Blue Notes and a former lead singer with the Elegants) teams with Kathy Marshall to provide a vocal duet with a unique style. Unforgettable has performed at the Pennsylvania Convention Center as the opening act for Shirley Jones, Bobby Rydell, the Drifters, Richard Simmons, Donald O'Connor, and the Platters. Edwards and Marshall have also appeared at President Bush's inaugural ball in Washington, D.C.; the MGM Grand, Excalibur, and Bellagio casinos in Las Vegas; the Waldorf Astoria in New York; and other venues in Pompano Beach and Ft. Lauderdale, Florida. The duet's repertoire features standards, Broadway show tunes, oldies, easy listening, and contemporary favorites.

Web site: www.unforgettablellc.com

JOE VALINO

Born and raised in South Philadelphia, Joe Valino reached the charts in 1956 with "Garden of Eden."

CHARLIE VENTURA

Born into a large music-loving family, Charlie Ventura was a skilled, up-tempo tenor saxophonist. Quitting his job at the Philadelphia Navy Yard during World War II, he joined Gene Krupa's band and became so popular during his time there that, in 1945, Ventura was voted best tenor saxophonist by *DownBeat* magazine. He later formed his own band and eventually signed a contract with RCA. For a brief period in the '50s, Ventura owned a nightclub in Philadelphia and created a popular combo known as the Big Four. He also continued his association with Krupa well into the '60s. In the '70s and '80s, he worked with various groups and spent time performing in Las Vegas.

THE VOLCANOS
Gene Jones (lead vocal), Steve Kelly (vocal), Harold "Doc" Wade (guitar), Stanley Wade (bass), John Hart (keyboard)

The Volcanos formed in 1964 and, by year's end, had released their first single: "Baby" (on Arctic Records). The following year, the group recorded "Storm Warning," which hit the national charts and became their biggest success. Subsequent releases: "Help Wanted" (composed by Gamble and Huff) and "(It's Against) The Laws of Love." In 1967, the Volcanos recorded two songs for Harthon Records: "It's Gotta Be a False Alarm" and "Take Me Back Again." Harold and Stanley Wade joined the Trammps in the early '70s.

CORKY WARREN

Beginning his career as an accomplished musician playing bass guitar, and singing backup for some of our most legendary rock and roll performers, Corky Warren has also served as honorary ringmaster for the Clyde Beatty/Cole Brothers Circus.

Since 1996, Warren has been an on-air personality for Quinn Broadcasting Television, simulcast on WMVB Radio and in recent years on WVLT 92.1 FM, where he also serves as musical director. His very popular weekly radio program, *Corky's Time Machine*, has mixed news and music of the past with his brand of comedy.

GEORGIE WOODS ("THE GUY WITH THE GOODS")

A legendary broadcasting personality in the City of Philadelphia, in a career that covered decades on WHAT and WDAS radio, Georgie Woods also staged legendary rock shows at the Uptown Theater in North Philadelphia and contributed much of his time to community needs. Along the way, Woods inspired many during his varied career in entertainment and public service.

◄ **Georgie Woods** became a renowned D.J. on the R&B airwaves and staged legendary music concerts at the Uptown Theater. *Courtesy Temple University Urban Archives*

▲ **Jocko Henderson** was said to have had one of the most unique and pleasant voices in the broadcasting industry. *Courtesy R&B Records*

► **Joe Grady and Ed Hurst,** *left to right,* in 1958. They started it all with the 950 Club on WPEN and became a fixture on radio and television for over 30 years. *Courtesy Ed Hurst*

◄ **Georgie Woods** rescues a young child knocked down by a group of fans in North Philadelphia in 1964. Throughout his long career in entertainment and public service, he inspired many. *Courtesy Temple University Urban Archives*

▶ **Jerry Blavat,** in 1960, when it all began for him. *Courtesy John Kinka*

▶ **Joe Niagara,** at WIBG in 1962. "Up there where the air is rare, this rockin' bird will fly." *Courtesy Joe Niagara Jr.*

◀ **Jerry Blavat,** today, is heard weekdays on the Geator Gold Radio Network in Philly and South Jersey. *Courtesy John Kinka*

◀ **Hy Lit,** in the '50s. He helped many recording artists in his travels "uptown, downtown, and crosstown." *Courtesy Lou Costello*

▲ **Hy Lit** Currently, "Hyski" is heard on the Web at hylitradio.com.

▲ **Joe Niagara and Hy Lit,** *left to right,* introduce Herman's Hermits and The Who at a 1968 Upper Darby concert. *Courtesy Joe Niagara Jr.*

▲ **King Arthur,** of WNJC, began his career in the late '60s doing local record hops, and a weekend radio show on WCAM. *Courtesy Janet Alvarez*

▲ **King Arthur,** in recent years. He remains a very popular radio host in the Delaware Valley. *Courtesy Janet Alvarez*

▲ **Bob Pantano,** circa 1977, at WCAU FM. He became an important part of the Delaware Valley music scene. *Courtesy Bob Pantano*

▲ **Christy Springfield** was a bright spot on Oldies 950 WPEN in 2005. *Courtesy Christy Springfield*

▲ **Bob Pantano,** today. As host of the popular *Saturday Night Dance Party,* he's pioneered the country's longest-running dance program. *Courtesy Bob Pantano*

▲ **Kal Rudman** began as a Top-40 D.J., then became *Billboard's* first R&B editor, and later created a nationally known music trade publication. *Courtesy Kal Rudman*

▲ **Jonathan P. Casey,** of WSNJ, vacations in California in between songs.
Courtesy Jonathan P. Casey

◄ **Tommy McCarthy** has been the music director at WOGL FM since 1993 and, more recently, began hosting a weekend TV show on the QBC-TV2 Cable Network. *Courtesy Tommy McCarthy*

► **Lou Costello** (known as the "Dancing D.J.") carries the memories of yesterday's music, heard daily on WVLT 92.1 FM, and also on his weekly Wednesday night show, the *Doo-Wop Diner. Courtesy Lou Costello*

▲ **Steve Kurtz** was recently heard weekly on WVLT playing rock and R&B from the '50s, '60s, and '70s. *Courtesy Steve Kurtz*

▲ **Val Shively** ("Emperor of the Oldies"), *right*, with veteran employee **Chuck Dabagian** at their R&B record store in Upper Darby. Their specialty shop is an amazing archive of 4 million vintage records, sold mostly through mail order to collectors all over the world. *Courtesy Val Shively*

▲ **Corky Warren** With a deep, rich, and distinctive vocal delivery, he hosts *Corky's Time Machine* on WVLT, blending news, comedy, and music. *Courtesy Lori Warren*

▲ **Jim Nettleton** has enjoyed a long-term relationship with the Philadelphia broadcast community, as an on-air personality, announcer, commercial spokesperson, and producer. *Courtesy Jim Nettleton*

▲ **Ali Hackett** ("King of the Oldies"). He was a long time D.J. on WHAT and, more recently, hosted a weekly show on WVLT, playing soul classics with a style and personality all his own. *Courtesy Ali Hackett*

▲ **The Four J's** Within a few months of being discovered by Buddy Greco, the group released their first charted hit, "Rock and Roll Age." They later traveled with Fabian and were known as the Fabulous Four. *Courtesy Jr. Pirollo*

▲ **The Larks** became a very popular '60s soul group. *Photo: Weldon A. McDougal III*

▲ **Anthony and the Sophomores** were a beloved group in 1960s Philadelphia, with hits like "Play Those Oldies Mr. D.J." and "Gee." *Courtesy Ernie Funaro*

▲ **Shirley Slaughter** A native Philadelphian, Slaughter first rose to prominence in the U.K., with hits such as "Real Love." *Photo: Weldon A. McDougal III*

◄ **Kenny Rossi** left *American Bandstand* at the height of his popularity to pursue a singing career. By the early 1960s, he had three charted hits and toured throughout the country. *Courtesy Arlene Sullivan*

160

▲ **Leon Mitchell** was the house bandleader at the Uptown Theater, from 1964 to 1974, where he worked with everyone who was anyone in R&B. *Courtesy Leon Mitchell*

▲ **Billy and the Essentials** Some of their most popular tunes were "The Dance Is Over," "Maybe You'll Be There," and "Over the Weekend." *Courtesy Billy Carlucci*

A Cappella Groups

The joy for us is returning to a time in the Philly neighborhoods when there were no barriers, and music was the universal language.

— Frank LaFaro

45 R.P.M.

Ted Ziffer (lead vocal, first tenor), Ernie Funaro (lead vocal, first tenor), Frank Caruso (second tenor), Chip Kopa (lead vocal, baritone), Lou Orsini (bass)

Formed to preserve street-corner harmony, 45 r.p.m. features songs from the '50s and '60s as well as vocal arrangements of more contemporary hits, with some tracks accompanied by preprogrammed instrumentation. (Ernie Funaro earlier performed with Anthony and the Sophomores.)

Web site: www.45rpmharmony.com

5/3 WOODLAND

Frank Maiorano (first tenor), Joe O'Connell (second tenor) Tom Tait (baritone), Al Loughead (baritone/bass)

Hailing from Southwest Philadelphia, the group 5/3 Woodland specializes in four-part harmony and has a diverse repertoire, ranging from primarily '50s and '60s to modern a cappella. Their latest CD: *It Ain't Easy.*

Web site: www.singers.com

CORNERSTONE

Harry Schmitt (lead vocal), Bill Diamond (tenor/ baritone), Pat Yocalano (tenor/baritone), Al Loughead (baritone/bass)

Cornerstone was formed in 2001 by the group's friend and manager Kenny "Oil Can" Patton. Led by veteran vocalist Harry Schmitt, Cornerstone has performed at premier doo-wop venues on the East and West coasts. Their latest CD, *Off the Corner*, recorded by Clifton Records, combines '50s R&B and classic group harmony.

Web site: www.welovedoowop.com

THE EMERALDS

Joe Porpora (founder, lead vocal), Jerry Tempesta (cofounder, first tenor), Jim DiPlacido (tenor, lead vocal), Scott Finlayson (baritone), Richie Grasso (bass, lead vocal)

Originating in the mid-'60s, the Emeralds sang on street corners, in the subway, and at the Concourse at City Hall. Rated one of the top a cappella groups in the Delaware Valley and New York area by their peers, the group specializes in recreating the original sound of the songs they perform. Their latest CD is *The Golden Sounds of the Emeralds.*

Web site: www.theemeralds.org

FRANKIE AND THE FASHIONS
Frank LaFaro (lead vocal), Henry Sauer (first tenor), Bill Hyde (second tenor), Mike Alullo (baritone)

Frankie and the Fashions were unique in that they performed a repertoire of original songs. Frank LaFaro has written over 50 tunes (in the doo-wop style), which have been recorded on over 10 CDs and have received airplay on oldies stations across the country. Their biggest hit is "What Do I Have to Do."

MEMORY LANE
Frankie Pescatore (first tenor), Frank LaFaro (tenor), Bobby Burgese (first tenor), John Poloney (baritone/bass), Richie Booker (second tenor)

In the versatile group, Memory Lane, each member sings lead and is capable of a wide vocal range. (Frank LaFaro is the former lead singer of Frankie and the Fashions.) The group's repertoire includes doo-wop classics, as well as more contemporary hits with a vocal group harmony flavor. Their current CD is entitled *Memory Lane/A Cappella Avenue* on the Collectables label.

Telephone: 215.551.3150, 215.603.8578

STREET CORNER FIVE
Rich Girese (lead vocal), Jim Bakay (first tenor), Dee Jaskel (second tenor), Mike Diamond (baritone), Bob Giordano (bass)

The group, Street Corner Five (managed by Ron Jaskel), celebrates the music of the '50s and '60s and enjoys involving their audience in reliving the joys of street-corner harmony. Their latest CD is *People Are Talking*.

Web site: www.streetcornerfive.blogspot.com

▲ **Frankie and the Fashions** performed a repertoire of original songs. Frank LaFaro (lead vocal) has written over 50 songs, recorded on over 10 CDs. *Courtesy Frank LaFaro*

◄ **Cornerstone** Led by veteran vocalist Harry Schmitt, Cornerstone combines '50s R&B and classic group harmony. *Courtesy Harry Schmitt*

▲ **The Emeralds** specialize in recreating the original sound of the songs they perform. *Courtesy Jerry Tempesta*

▲ **45 r.p.m.** features songs from the '50s and '60s, as well as vocal arrangements of more contemporary hits. *Courtesy Ernie Funaro*

ENDNOTES

Chapter 1
Rhythm and Blues *The Early Years*
1. Lou Costello, interview by the author, telephone, Vineland, New Jersey, July 2005.
2. Leon Mitchell, interview by the author, telephone, Philadelphia, Pennsylvania, August 2005.

Chapter 2
Rock 'n' Roll *A New Variation*
1. Weldon Arthur McDougal III, interview by the author, Upper Darby, Pennsylvania, July 2005.
2. Lee Andrews, interview by the author, East Lansdowne, Pennsylvania, July 2005.
3. Costello, interview.
4. Bob Bosco, interview by the author, telephone, Philadelphia, Pennsylvania, July 2005.
5. James Darren, interview by the author, telephone, Los Angeles, California, July 2004.
6. Charlie Gracie, interview by the author, telephone, Upper Darby, Pennsylvania, June 2004.
7. Al "Caesar" Berry, interview by the author, Philadelphia, Pennsylvania, July 2004.

Chapter 3
Philly in the British and Motown Years
1. Joe Tarsia, interview by the author, Haddonfield, New Jersey, August 2005.
2. Bunny Sigler, interview by the author, Philadelphia, Pennsylvania, July 2005.
3. David J. Steinberg, interview by the author, telephone, Bala Cynwyd, Pennsylvania, August 2005.
4. Jonathan P. Casey, interview by the author, telephone, Cape May, New Jersey, August 2005.
5. Stephen Caldwell, interview by the author, telephone, Philadelphia, Pennsylvania, July 2005.
6. Jerry Blavat, interview by the author, telephone, Philadelphia, Pennsylvania, August 2005.
7. Andrews, interview.
8. Joe Terry, interview by the author, Williamstown, New Jersey, July 2005.
9. McDougal, interview.
10. Ali Hackett, interview by the author, Philadelphia, Pennsylvania, July 2005.
11. Charlie and Richie Ingui, interview by the author, Marlton, New Jersey, August 2005.
12. Ken Jeremiah, interview by the author, Atlantic City, New Jersey, July 2005.

Chapter 4
The Maestro and the Lyricist
1. Thom Bell, interview by the author, telephone, Washington State, August 2005.
2. William "Poogie" Hart, interview by the author, Cheltenham, Pennsylvania, July 2005.
3. DIDN'T I (BLOW YOUR MIND THIS TIME)
  Words and Music by THOMAS BELL and WILLIAM HART
  Copyright 1970(Renewed) WARNER-TAMERLANE PUBLISHING CORP.
  All Rights Reserved Used by Permission
4. Steven Epstein, interview by the author, Dresher, Pennsylvania, July 2005.
5. Russell Thompkins Jr., interview by the author, Philadelphia, Pennsylvania, June 2005.
6. PEOPLE MAKE THE WORLD GO ROUND
  Words and Music by THOM BELL and LINDA CREED
  Copyright 1974(Renewed) WARNER-TAMERLANE PUBLISHING CORP.
  All Rights Reserved Used by Permission
7. Andrews, interview.

Chapter 5
The Sound of Philadelphia
1. Tarsia, interview.
2. Billy Paul, interview by the author, telephone, Philadelphia, Pennsylvania, August 2005.
3. Lawrence Brown, interview by the author, Philadelphia, Pennsylvania, July 2005.
4. Lloyd Parks, interview by the author, Wildwood, New Jersey, August 2005.
5. Sigler, interview.
6. Harold Watkins, interview by the author, telephone, Philadelphia, Pennsylvania, July 2005.
7. Jimmy Ellis, interview by the author, telephone, South Carolina, July 2005.
8. Ed Cermanski, interview by the author, telephone, Conshohocken, Pennsylvania, July 2005.

ABOUT THE AUTHOR

Courtesy The Reporter

Born and raised in Northwest Philadelphia, James Rosin graduated from Temple University's School of Communications with a degree in broadcasting. In New York, he studied acting with Bobby Lewis and appeared in plays off-off Broadway and on the ABC soap opera, *Edge of Night*. In Los Angeles, Rosin played featured and costarring roles in such TV shows as *Mike Hammer; T. J. Hooker; Quincy M.E.; General Hospital; The Powers of Matthew Star; Cannon; Mannix; Banacek; Adam-12; Love, American Style;* and two miniseries, *Loose Change* and *Once an Eagle*. He also wrote stories and teleplays for *Quincy M.E.* (NBC), *Capitol* (CBS), and *Loving Friends and Perfect Couples* (Showtime). His full-length play, *Michael in Beverly Hills,* premiered at Don Eitner's American Theater Arts in Los Angeles and was later presented off-off Broadway at the American Musical Dramatic Academy's Studio One Theater.

In recent years, Rosin has written and produced two one-hour sports documentaries, which have aired on public television: *Philly Hoops: The SPHAS and Warriors* (about the first two professional basketball teams in Philadelphia) and *The Philadelphia Athletics 1901–1954* (about the former American League franchise). His first book, *Philly Hoops: The SPHAS and Warriors*, was published in October of 2003. His second book, *Rock, Rhythm & Blues,* came out in September 2004.